always coming back home

always coming back home

An Emotional Tale
of Love, Adventure,
Tragedy and Hope

ASHLEY BUGGE

NEW YORK
LONDON • NASHVILLE • MELBOURNE • VANCOUVER

Always Coming Back Home

An Emotional Tale of Love, Adventure, Tragedy and Hope

Published in New York, New York, by Morgan James Publishing. Morgan James is a trademark of Morgan James, LLC. www.MorganJamesPublishing.com

ISBN 9781642799088 paperback
ISBN 9781642799095 eBook
Library of Congress Control Number: 2019954708

Cover Design by:
Megan Dillon
megan@creativeninjadesigns.com

Interior Design by:
Christopher Kirk
www.GFSstudio.com

This book is dedicated to Isabel, Hudson, and Adeline in memory of your Dad, Brian James Bugge. I hope these stories give you a glimpse into the incredible life he lived and the love we shared that brought each of you into this world.

Brian, I miss you terribly.

Table of Contents

Acknowledgments

Isabel, Hudson and Adeline. You are my inspiration, my motivation and my encouragement. Without knowing it, you have saved me in more ways than one and I'm so unbelievably proud of you, I love you.

Brunella, your support and dedication in helping me tell my story has made this book possible and I'm grateful, here's to book number two and beyond!

To Linda and Robert, I would not have made it through 20 May without you. Thank you for answering your phone.

To Uncle Mike, thank you for answering his Craigslist ad and for the countless kitchen singalongs.

To Nikki for never leaving my side.

To Mama T and Gpa, for raising the man I fell in love with.

To Mom, Dad, Pat, Zack, Kellie, Ben, Jenn, Will, Aaron, Elliot, Kaius, John, Tom, Stacie, Jess, Kasey, Timi, George, Meg, Matt T, Brian N, Matt B, Nick, Katy, Aunt Sharon, Erika, Beau, Lara, Peter, Chris R, Myley, Melanie and Brae, thank you for loving Brian and flying to a rock in the middle of the ocean to hold my hand as we said goodbye.

To David C, for helping me understand.

To my friends in the PNW who make this place feel like home, who dropped everything to welcome us back, and for being Aunties & Uncles to my three kids. I'm indebted to you.

A special thank you to former Stay Gold crew and especially Chris, Willy and Beau who spent twenty-one days on a yellow sailboat in order to make a dream come true for Brian.

To V, Kay and NeeNee, you were there when we needed you most.

To the Navy for supporting my family through this entire ordeal, specifically you, Nate.

To the diving and sailing communities around the world who have embraced us as one of your own.

To Morgan James Publishing for wanting this story told and giving me the platform to tell it.

Lastly, to Brian. You are the reason for this. You are the man of my dreams and the love of my life; I'll forever be grateful for our time together and how you encouraged me to live life and take chances like this. If you fall asleep down by the water, baby I'll carry you all the way home.

I love you.

Introduction

E Komo Mai. It means *Welcome* in Hawaiian. It's what people walking by our house on Bridges Street of Joint Base Pearl Harbor–Hickam would see posted on our front door. We bought this sign when we first moved to Honolulu, Hawaii, on military orders in the summer of 2017. To say that our little wooden sign was hanging by a thread would be an understatement. Every time the screen door closed a bit too hard, the little palm tree on the right-hand side of the Hawaiian greeting fell off. Rather than spend another seven dollars on a new sign from the Navy Exchange, we opted to continuously glue the poor palm tree back on more times than I can count. The kitchen junk drawer glue offering a temporary fix, until it came crashing down again.

Our house was dark brown with light brown trim, and Brian and I fell in love with it the first time we pulled in the driveway. After living in the Ford Island Navy Lodge hotel for sixty-one nights, I was elated when Brian called to tell me a home in the military base housing had become available and we could view it the next day. The moment we pulled into the driveway, we were greeted by a welcoming sight: two stunning Birds of Paradise plants at the entrance to our front porch. With their beautiful banana-shaped leaves and bright orange and intense blue flowers, Birds of Paradise have been a symbol of Oahu—and my favorite flower—for as long as I can remember. As we stood together on that front porch waiting to see the inside of this house, the trade winds whooshed over us, bringing through warm fragrant smells of the nearby ocean, and swaying the trunk of the giant palm tree across the street. These winds we would come to love, swirled all around us, rattling the screen door and whispering *E Komo Mai*. A simple and single sign that we were living in paradise. Brian and I looked at each other, smiling. We were home.

We woke up early the morning of May 20, 2018, because Brian had a scuba diving class to get to. He loved diving and had started taking lessons from a nearby dive shop on how to use a closed-circuit rebreather. The rebreather is a breathing apparatus used in advanced recreational and technical deep diving. This device absorbs the carbon dioxide of the breather and recycles it by allowing the user to essentially rebreathe the unused oxygen using a closed-circuit loop. It is a complicated machine to put together, as it requires undivided attention and careful assemblage. Brian had stayed up late the previous night, spending over an hour in the garage getting his rebreather ready for the upcoming class. Satisfied with the result, he came to bed, kissed me good night, and got some rest.

The warm sunrays peeking through our window blinds reminded us that a brand-new day had just risen in paradise. I squinted, stretched my arms over my head, and got up slowly, as my six-month-old pregnant belly made it hard for me to go anywhere fast. Brian was already awake, trying to stay quiet as he got ready for his morning adventure, but the telltale light and scent of his tea tree shampoo coming from under the door of our bathroom let me know he'd be a few more minutes. He finally emerged, jumping into bed to kiss my pregnant belly and I good morning, before we made our way downstairs. We held hands and tiptoed down the hall, trying to be as quiet as possible so that our two children, Isabel and Hudson, would stay asleep. As most parents of young children can attest to, we had learned which floorboards caused the most noise and were willing to go to great lengths to avoid them in order to keep the kids sleeping as long as possible on those weekend mornings. After a quick cup of coffee together, Brian assured me he'd let me know when he had surfaced from his dive. We always had a plan before he left for these dives, so I knew where he'd be diving, who he'd be diving with, and what time to expect to hear from him. This Sunday morning was no different and I knew that, after his boat dive, he'd be headed to the pool for more training and that I should hear from him no later than noon. Brian and I exchanged *I love you*'s and I kissed my husband goodbye.

I watched him walk toward his white pickup truck—the Island Beater we had purchased more or less to haul his diving equipment around in—and I smiled to myself. With our two beautiful babies sleeping upstairs and our third doing cartwheels in my belly, I was a lucky girl and a proud wife. Brian was an adventurer, an explorer, and, since I wasn't able to partake in diving while pregnant, I was looking forward to hearing about his adventure that morning. He'd be diving a familiar sight: a sunken ship called the *Sea Tiger*, a former Chinese vessel named *Yun Fong Seong* located west of

Waikiki at about ninety feet deep into the blue waters of Oahu. I could already hear the excitement in his voice as he replayed everything he had seen under water, always recalling it using the Hawaiian names for the animals: *tako* (octopus), *honu* (sea turtle), and sometimes *nai'a* (dolphins).

A light, warm, humid breeze coming from the ocean helped ease Brian's truck out of the driveway as we waved our final goodbyes for the morning. It traveled through our front yard, dancing across the coconut trees and flowers, before greeting me with that exotic, energizing smell I'd come to know as the scent of home. It was those same trade winds we'd witnessed on our first day on Bridges Street that brought through smells of coffee from the neighbors' houses, along with suntan lotion from the community pool and salt from the nearby surfers' waves. Inhaling it all in with a deep breath, I turned around to walk back upstairs, when the creaking sound of the screen door closing sent me into panic mode—that panic any parent with small children can relate to. The panic when you know that something is about to cause enough noise to wake up your little ones, who have been sleeping peacefully. These little ones you work so hard to get to fall asleep in the first place, only to wake up if the wind hits the shutter the wrong way, or someone—three houses down—coughs too loud. That same panic that turns you into an aspiring gold medal gymnast in your own living room as you do flips and kicks through the air just to avoid that door from slamming shut. This particular morning, I watched my dreams of making the Olympic podium crash as I was too little too late . . . the screen door went *swoosh*, the kids awoke from their slumber and, obviously, the Hawaiian greeting sign went *thud!*

"Oh, good grief . . ." I mumbled under my breath as I walked into the kitchen in search of the glue.

A few moments later, I heard little footsteps coming down the stairs. I stopped searching the junk drawer, looked up toward the staircase, and saw the sun-bleached messy hair sticking out from the kitchen counter.

"Good morning, Izzy," I said, walking toward my daughter to give her a hug. She melted in my arms and snuggled her face into my neck, trying to protect her sleepy eyes from the bright sunlight. At three years old, Izzy already had plenty of personality and was a ball of unfiltered (hilarious) commentary. I picked her up—not an easy task when you have a giant belly to manage as well—and walked the three of us to the bright red couch in our living room. I turned the TV on and began the morning argument of which show to watch: Izzy voted for the Disney movie *Moana* (for the millionth time), but soon became distracted by her assortment of toys littering our living room floor, so I scrolled through our Netflix account to find *Blue Planet*, a documentary series focused on the marine environment of Earth. Soon after settling in, we were joined by the little man of the house. Hudson made his way downstairs, trailed only by his constant companion: a twelve-inch light brown bear that my mother had gifted him when he was born over a year ago. We had never come up with a nickname for this ragged stuffed animal, instead just referring to it as Bear. The name stuck and Hudson never let Bear out of his sight.

After a solid hour of Sunday-morning couch snuggles, the kids and I decided it was time to start our day. We had big things planned, including going to Target to shop for newborn clothes and spending the afternoon with Brian. Izzy loved any excuse to go on a shopping date to Target, but today she was excited about being able to choose clothes for her little sister. Hudson, on the other hand, was just along for the ride and was happy to be joining us girls as long as it meant he could bring Bear with him. It was never less than eighty degrees outside, so we all got dressed in very light clothes: I put on my favorite maternity jean shorts, the same shorts that had seen each of my previous pregnancies, as well as a navy blue tank top, and my flip-flops—or *slippahs*, as the locals called them. The slippahs were black with a white turtle drawing and the word *Aloha* written across the top. They were one of my first and favorite purchases to date that I had made since moving to Oahu. These slippahs had seen thunderstorms, dive boats, doctor's offices, family beach days, and three of the Hawaiian Islands. With the exception of a weeklong family trip to Japan in February, these slippahs had not left my side or my feet in nine months.

By 8:30 a.m., the kids were dressed, and we were almost ready to go. At six months pregnant, pregnancy brain was in full swing, so I went through my mental checklist of things to remember before leaving the house: Kids, check. Keys, check. Wallet, check. Reusable Target bags, check. I was actually quite proud of myself for remembering this last one as plastic bags are banned in the city of Honolulu, so you have to bring your own recyclable bags when you go shopping. Target just so happens to sell them at their checkout stand for those who forget and has also earned no less than an entire paycheck from my family alone on these bags. I had a wide variety to choose from as I rifled through our pantry, beaming with pride that I'd save the ninety-nine cents from having to buy yet another reusable bag on this shopping trip.

Kids, purse, keys, bags.

Content with the knowledge I had everything I needed for the morning, I piled it all on the kitchen island and ran to the TV room to blow out the vanilla coconut candle Brian had gifted me for Mother's Day the weekend before. Just as I had set everything down, my phone rang. *Uh, now what?* I thought. I rifled through my purse, feeling blindly through bags of kids' fruit snacks and plastic toy cars for my phone to see who was calling me. It was a number I didn't know. *Weird.* I rarely answer the phone if I don't know the number because I just can't stand all of the sales calls. With two young children at home, I had plenty of opportunity for people to talk my ear off; I didn't need it from random salespeople as well—especially on this beautiful Sunday morning. Yet, this call was different. Something inside me told me to answer that call. I knew Brian was in the water and, just like every single deployment we'd been through throughout his naval career, when your husband is in a potentially dangerous situation and he doesn't have direct access to a phone, every military wife will tell you, you answer those calls from numbers you don't know.

"Kids, *shhh.*" I brought my index finger to my lips looking at Izzy and Hudson, who were so excited about going out they couldn't contain their enthusiasm and were rather high pitched. "Hey, mama has to answer the phone real quick, OK?"

They looked at me and I could see my words hadn't registered with them. So, I went ahead and just answered the call.

"Hello?"

"Mrs. Bugge?" an unfamiliar voice asked. The male voice sounded as if he was out of breath, a distinct note of concern penetrated through the phone line. *Well, this doesn't sound like a sales call,* I thought to myself.

"Yes, this is she," I replied slowly, with a questioning tone that implied *Why are you calling me?*

"I'm calling from the dive shop, there's been an accident involving your husband Brian, where are you right now?"

Pause.

Accident. Involving. My. Husband.

Motionless.

Time paused.

It stood still.

My brain had a hard time processing these words.

The excited screams of my two little children brought me back to reality.

"I . . . I am . . . I'm home, what's going on?"

"There's been an accident on the dive boat I need to know your address I'm coming to get you." His words came out as if in one single breath and if somebody had pressed fast-forward on a recorded speech.

"NO!" I screamed as the color left my face, a lump rising in my throat. "No, no, no!"

"Yes, Mrs. Bugge, we are coming to get you. Where are you? Are you at home? Do you have your kids with you? We need your address."

"STOP!" I yelled, now breathless, "No, please stop!"

I looked down at my children, our children. They looked up at me, equally concerned. In that moment, every ounce of energy left my body. I had no idea what had happened to my Brian, but one thing I knew for sure: there are no second chances in the water.

Chapter One

January 2013
Portland, Oregon

I sat nervously in the black leather swivel chair nestled behind my banker's desk. Tokens from my travels around the world scattered in front of me: A hand-carved wooden hippo from Botswana, a small tin Eiffel Tower key chain from France, and a white ceramic mug I'd bought in Italy filled with the stale coffee I'd been too anxious to drink since I'd received his text message that morning. Looking at them on my desk reminded me of the incredible adventures I'd been on, and also served as a calming presence to my clients, as well as myself, in tense situations at the bank. I looked at them and tried to calm myself down, but even daydreams of faraway places and adventures waiting to happen couldn't distract me today. My left leg twitching, shaking, and finally bouncing up and down as I tried to appear composed to the row of tellers looking over at me. I had been held up in a bank robbery six years prior, yet somehow, I felt more nervous in this exact moment than I remember feeling then. I was waiting for a phone call that I knew was about to change the course of my entire life.

I hadn't heard his voice in over nine years. Powerful and commanding, yet kind and gentle. A voice that stands out in a room of people, but also draws you in for long one-on-one conversations. I looked at my phone watching the minutes tick on, waiting to hear this voice from my past once again: 10:26; 10:27; 10:28. I wasn't *technically* supposed to have my phone on my desk while working at the bank, but the text messages we had exchanged that morning led me to believe this phone call was worth potentially getting reprimanded at work for. I nestled it between the pages of my 2013 yearly planner and pretended to be thoroughly sketching out my January appointments—instead watching intently as the minutes passed by: 10:29; 10:30; 10:31. His last text message had asked if he could give me a call on his lunch break and I hadn't heard from him since responding, "yes!" What time did people in the Navy eat lunch anyways?

Tick tock: 10:32; 10:33; 10:34 . . . 10:34! My phone exploded in sound from its place between my calendar pages. *Here we go!* I ripped that calendar cover open as quickly as humanly possible, grabbed my phone, and sprinted toward the break room door. My hand reached for the pewter-colored door handle and pressed down. LOCKED? Dang it! I knew from years of experience it would take me a solid fifteen seconds to sort through my numerous keys to find the right one that would open this solid wooden door. I hit the talk button, took a deep breath, willing myself to play it cool, and pulled the phone to my ear.

"Hello?" The elongated sound of the second syllable *-llooooo* ending in a high-pitched tone totally gave away the fact that I was both nervous and incredibly overjoyed about talking to him. So much for playing it cool. I'm sure he could picture the big smile that spread across my entire face. I found the right key and opened the break room door just as he responded.

"Hey Ashley, it's Brian." That same voice from all those years ago. He sounded older, more mature, but I could hear the smile on his face too.

"Hey! It's been FOREVER! How are you?"

"I'm good!" he said confidently, pausing for a moment before resuming. "Actually, if I can speak honestly, I'm just OK."

"Just OK?" I fished, already having an idea of what was happening in his personal life that had prompted his reaching out to me after so long. "What's wrong?" I continued, anxious to hear.

"Well"—he paused briefly—"a lot has happened since we last talked, but I guess the first thing I should tell you is that I'm getting divorced." He sounded conflicted. Sad, but happy. Cautious, but hopeful. The Brian I remembered wasn't a quitter nor did he accept failure, but I could hear in his voice this decision was final.

"Oh no! I'm so sorry," I lied. The smile spreading even more across my face.

"Yeah . . . well, let's talk about something else. How are you?"

"I'm so happy to be talking to you, I can't believe it's been this long. You sound exactly the same as I remember." My cheeks hurt from smiling so hard. I had thought about this moment—the potential for this phone call—so many times over the previous nine years, I couldn't believe this was happening and he was on the other end of that line.

I was anxious, but at ease in talking to him. We were both on our best behaviors, trying to sum up the lives we'd led independent of each other while apart. We talked about how I, too, had been married, how it had ended in divorce a few years earlier, and how, since then, I'd been working, traveling, and finishing my bachelor's degree and EMT license. At times throughout this call, my coworkers would come in to grab coffee or water, glancing at me with questioning eyes and curious smiles, wanting to know who could possibly be causing me to blush so severely in that frigid back room.

"So, how about you?" I asked him cautiously. I knew he had a story to tell—and I was anxious to hear it—but I already had a feeling this phone call wouldn't be our last and he would fill me in once he was comfortable doing so.

"I bought a sailboat last year so that's been keeping me busy."

"Wait, whaaaat?!" I interrupted him. "You know how to sail?! Dude. I learned how to sail a few years ago too!"

"No way!" He was just as surprised. "Work sent me to Virginia a couple of years ago and instead of going out drinking with the guys, I rented a little Hobie Cat and taught myself how to sail. I loved it so much I came home and traded in my motorcycle for a sailboat." I could hear the excitement in his voice as he started telling me about his boat. "I have it moored here in Gig Harbor, Washington, and try to go out on it every weekend I'm home."

"That's amazing!" I could barely contain my joy. I adjusted myself on the impossibly hard plastic chair I'd been sitting in, and told him, "I got my ASA 101 Basic Keelboat certification through the sailing school I was working at in Portland, Oregon." I went on to tell him, "After leaving New York City, I moved back here and saw this job posting saying they needed somebody to run the sailing school office. They couldn't pay much, but they'd teach me to sail and I could use the boats whenever I wanted. Fun. Adventure. Water. It sounded right up my alley, so I applied, and they hired me on the spot."

"That's so wild. You should come up here sometime and we can go out on my boat, *Time and Tide*."

That smile crept back on my face as the thought of Brian and me out on his boat in the middle of the Puget Sound swept through my mind. "That's a cool name for a boat," I commented. "Time and tide wait for no man," he responded. "It seemed appropriate for her." It took less than an instant for me to respond with "Absolutely, I'd love that!" I giggled to myself at the thought of the two of us, relatively young—we were both in our early thirties—and heavily tattooed, in the middle of the Puget Sound on a sailboat. It would be quite the sight for all of the seasoned salty sailors in that uppity little coastal town, but the thought was making us both happy and we exploded in laughter. We continued to talk, sharing stories of mutual friends, trips around the world each of us had taken, pets, family, and where life had led us since we'd last spoken.

"Anyway," he said, "I'm so sorry to say this, but I have to go back to work."

I didn't know how long we'd been on the phone, but I knew I had far exceeded an appropriate length of break time in that back room.

"Yeah, me too . . ." Drawing out my words because I didn't want to say goodbye. I was sad to let him go, but we both knew we couldn't possibly stay on the phone any longer. I just wasn't ready for it to end though, and I could tell he felt the same way. Was it possible to have a crush on someone you haven't talked to in this long? My palms were sweating, my foot was twitching, and the butterflies in my stomach were trying to find a way out. I felt this urge raising from deep inside me and, before I could even process the words, I just blurted out, "Hey, so I know we haven't seen each other in nine years, but would you like to come with me to Costa Rica for my birthday? I have this whole trip planned and I'd love it if you could—"

"Yes! I'd love to!"

I sat up straight.

Did that just happen?! I was shocked, not sure if more at myself for just inviting him on the trip, or if at him for accepting.

"Sweet!" I exclaimed while mouthing the words OH MY GOD to the empty room. "Have a good rest of your day at work, I'll talk to you later."

We said goodbye and vowed to talk again that evening. Nine years was a long time, and we had a lot more of catching up to do.

Ninety minutes of sitting in a cheap white plastic chair on a hard tile floor had created a handful of knots in my body, but I stood up, shook out my limbs, stretched my back, and floated on cloud nine out of that break room. As soon as I opened the solid wooden door entering back into the bank lobby, my boss Anita started walking toward me with a purpose. I could tell by the wink she gave me, and the fact that she grabbed my wrists pulling me into her office, she wasn't mad. On the contrary, she was itching to know all about my call.

"OK, so who was that?!" she asked in her thick West Virginian accent, eyebrows raised, and with a tone telling me I wasn't leaving her office until she had the full scoop.

"It was Brian." The frown on her forehead reminded me she didn't know about him. "Brian. BJ. Bugge. Anita, I can't believe it. He was my boyfriend a decade ago, and we spoke for the first time in nine years today! I know this is crazy, but I swear to you, I think I'm going to marry him."

"Your boyfriend? Marry him!? What?? Oh, Ashley, bless your heart. I need to know everything!"

****

Portland, Oregon. 2002.

My older brother, Zack, had joined the Army and was currently deployed in response to the terrorist attacks on September 11, 2001. Zack and I had grown very close since our parents had divorced, and he would always let me tag along with him to the punk-rock concerts that Portland was known for at the time. He and his friends were in bands and always playing shows in smoke- and graffiti-filled venues in the up-and-coming parts of town—before they were actually up and coming. He'd bring me with him when he was supposed to be babysitting me, introducing me to his friends with the implicit instructions to "stay away from my little sister," so much so that the only person allowed to hang out with me was Tom, his best friend since third grade and my surrogate-type brother while Zack was away. During this time of Zack being deployed, Tom lived in a house on the corner of South-East 49th and Division street in Portland with a handful of friends and bandmates, all young guys and all people my big brother had advised me to stay far, far away from. Obviously, I didn't listen. Tom had invited me over to watch their band practice and, naturally, I invited a couple of my girlfriends to come with me. We walked down the basement stairs to their practice space, the smell of sweat, mold, and the dirty laundry of a bunch of heavily tattooed twenty-ish-year-old young men hitting us before we reached the bottom step. My girlfriends, who were not interested in the same type of music I was at the time, put on a brave face and suffered through what they would probably describe as loud noise filtering out of the practice space. I listened and watched intently, proud of these people I called friends for doing something they loved: playing music and screaming out handwritten lyrics that meant something to each of them. They finished up and Tom started introducing everyone.

"Ashley, this is BJ."

"Hi," I said, shaking his hand. "Nice to meet you."

He smiled but seemed very shy. I couldn't help but think he was really cute, especially that dimple that appeared on his left cheek as he smiled at me. A tall, chubby kid with bright blue eyes and swooping black hair who I was told lived upstairs in the attic of this house. He was known among our friends for loving the Cure and *Band of Brothers*, giving great hugs, and for being the front man of two local punk bands, Inked in Blood and West of Zero.

I was living in Olympia, Washington, at the time, working on my bachelor's degree at the Evergreen State College so I didn't see Brian again until I was down visiting on Christmas break, yet I found myself thinking of his handsome face and bright blue eyes from time to time. Since we had so many mutual friends, we kept in touch via AOL instant messenger (referred to as AIM at the time) and a website called LiveJournal—think Myspace/Facebook in their infant stages. By the spring of 2003, a handful of our friends had started working for a local Portland company called CD Baby. Every time I was in town, I'd head to CD Baby with the excuse I wanted to go visit a girlfriend, Michelle, who also worked there; however, I was quite transparent, and everyone knew I was really going to see him.

Even though his office was at the front of the store, whenever I was there, he would somehow find a way to come into the back room where Michelle spent her days copying CDs onto a computer. He'd sit and eat Slim Jim beef jerky sticks, drink Ruby Red Squirt, and chat with me for as long as I was willing to stay at their workplace. I knew he was developing a crush on me, but I wasn't sure if I was there yet. I was certainly intrigued though. He was the sweetest and most genuine guy from our group of friends, probably in Portland, and possibly all of Oregon, if I'm being really honest. Brian was so shy, so unaware of how handsome and funny he was. Truly humble and unassuming. We spent hours chatting with each other from afar on AIM and, as time went by, I couldn't help the butterflies in my stomach as I thought of him.

xashleyporschex: ATTN: BJ. I just called you, but you didn't answer your phone. I hope that means you are doing something exciting to celebrate your birthday. Like Chuck E Cheese or something like that. Go jump in that ball pit! That thing rules!! HAPPY BIRTHDAY.

100yearsofblood: I wish I was in the ball pit! But, I'm not. Oh well, there's always next year, or maybe Aug 4th. Who knows. All I know is you're a doll. There's more to say, but not today, maybe someday. <3 you.

One day, while I was at Tom's house, I decided it was time. Overly confident in a way only a twenty-year-old can be, I walked upstairs to Brian's bedroom to say hi and to do some flirting.

"I'm about to watch *Of Mice and Men*," he said. "Have you seen it before?"

"Heck yes, it's one of my favorite movies!" It's possible I had heard of the movie before, but I'd certainly never seen it and it was a far cry from the usual documentary or slapstick type movie my friends and I usually watched. I'm not sure why I lied, but I am sure I would have used any excuse to sit next to him on that little black futon in the sweltering attic he lived in and if BJ wanted to watch *Of Mice and Men* then this was going to be my favorite movie today.

"Do you wanna watch it with me?" he asked.

"Sure," I said. Again, overly confident, but I could feel my heartbeat started rising a bit.

We sat as awkwardly as possible on that futon and watched this terribly sad movie, all the while each of us wishing the other would make a move. Our hands moved slowly toward each other and, at one point, I thought for sure he was going to put his arm around me as an invitation to cuddle, but it didn't happen. He was too shy, and I was still working out my feelings for him. However, I didn't have to wait long. Soon after that, he would ask me to be his girlfriend.

The first date he asked me on went something like this: "So, umm . . . I was thinking of going down to the coast on Friday night, just walking around Fort Stevens and hanging out for a little bit . . ." Then, there was a long pause on his part, quite obviously either waiting to build up the courage to ask if I wanted to go with him, or possibly waiting for me to invite myself. It's been so long since that date, I can't quite remember which way it went, but I do remember what we each wore on our trip down to the Oregon Coast, how special I felt being with him while exploring the old fort, laughing uncontrollably, taking pictures on the jetty, singing along to the Smashing Pumpkins song "Tonight, Tonight," and the butterflies I felt in the pit of my stomach when he grabbed my hand on the drive home in his little blue two-door car. I still have a photo from this first date sitting on my bedside table as I type this, and I still have that ratty old San Francisco sweatshirt hanging in my closet.

Since our first date, and a very special photo I took for Brian pre-deployment, I haven't worn that sweatshirt again; yet, I have never been able to get rid of it, not even during the decade we spent apart, because it reminds me of this one night with him at the Oregon Coast, one of the most special nights of my life. From that day on, and for the next six weeks in the summer of 2003, I was able to call Brian—the shy yet charming boy who lived in the attic—my boyfriend. We spent the summer together, swimming and cliff jumping at Dougan Falls, laughing with friends at concerts, celebrating each other's birthdays, watching movies in his attic apartment, and making trips down to the coast, a place that would forever become a part of our love story.

I'd say I knew Brian had fallen for me within about three weeks—and he'd fallen hard. He was only twenty-two years old, and I was one year younger than him; yet, he knew exactly what he wanted. He started talking about his plans to join the Coast Guard and how we could get married and live at the coast—any coast. He spent hours talking about the life we could have together. Marriage, kids, careers, a dog, maybe two. He had a vision and was serious. I could barely figure out where my friends and I would be going for dinner that night, let alone where I wanted to be in a year, five years, ten years from then. But Brian didn't have a doubt. He saw me in his future, and he was ready to build his entire life around us. I knew Brian was the perfect man, and I was certain he was going to be the perfect partner. However, at only twenty-one years old, I also knew I wasn't ready for all of that. He was the right guy, but it was the wrong time.

I made the call and asked him to come over to talk. I could feel the blood pumping through my veins as my palms became sweaty. I was nervous. I knew he was all in, and I also knew I was about to break his heart. The anticipation was building up inside of me to the point that when I asked him to go for a walk, I was having a hard time walking at his same pace, often finding myself ahead of him and having to stop and wait for him to catch up.

"Are you OK?" He felt something was wrong.

"Ehm . . ." I had spent hours trying to find the right words. I knew what I was about to say was going to be rough. Weighing words wasn't going to cushion the blow. So, I just blurted it out in one breath: "I think we need to take a break."

Silence. His black Converse sneakers coming to an abrupt halt on the sidewalk.

"I think we should just be friends." I added salt to the wound. I did my best to explain I really liked him, but I wasn't at the same place in my life as he was. He asked if we could just slow it down and he'd stop talking about the future, but my mind was made up. He took it all in and respected my decision without fighting against it, something that made me admire him even more.

Months went by, and we didn't talk to each other at all. I knew he was hurt, and I knew my continuing to reach out would be confusing for us both. Eventually, I heard through the grapevine that he had joined the Navy and he was getting ready to ship off to boot camp. He was now a military man and would be known going forward in his career as STS1 Brian J Bugge; a sonartech on submarines. I was invited to his going-away party on November 25, 2003. It was great to see him looking so happy. We gave each other hugs, said our goodbyes, and he left for uncharted waters.

We kept in loose contact from that point on while he was in basic training and eventually his first duty station in Groton, Connecticut. As time went on, we began writing more often to each other. I had recently purchased a house with my little brother, Ben, in Fruit Valley, Washington, and I would spend evenings sitting on a wooden bench we had by the back door, under the glow of the single porch light, writing him long love letters while listening to the Weezer song "Across the Sea" on repeat. In the summer of 2004, he surprised me by sending me a bouquet of Birds of Paradise to the Veterans Administration hospital I worked for. The first bouquet of flowers I'd ever had delivered to me at work and probably the most meaningful even to this day. "Wish I could be there to have fun with you! Have an amazingly fun day!! I miss you. Love, Brian James." I read this inscription, blushing and beaming at the same time at the thoughtful gesture. I remember my coworkers gushing over it and even my mom saying she had never received flowers as beautiful as these before. They sat on the entryway to my house for weeks—long after I should have thrown them away—because the thought behind them made me so happy, and I couldn't bring myself to get rid of them.

Brian took my breath away when he came to visit me that summer in my little house in Fruit Valley. He had finished boot camp, had lost about fifty pounds, had a handful of new tattoos paying tribute to his admiration of the sea, and he carried himself with more confidence than the shy boy who had left town the previous fall. He wasn't sure yet where he would be heading next, but we spent our few days together making it count. He lost his virginity on that visit, an experience that was scary but exhilarating and exciting—a theme that would play out time and time again throughout our romance and lives together.

Eventually, we started to lose touch again and the letters and phone calls became fewer and further between. The next thing I knew, I heard from my stepsister Jessica that he had gotten married. I remember getting that phone call and falling back on the light blue velvet couch in my living room, arms outstretched, palms up, looking at the mirror attached to our TV stand, and thinking *that's it, I've lost my chance.*

****

Anita couldn't believe the story of how Brian and I had met, what we had been through together, and the fact that we were back in each other's lives after over a decade of silence.

"Ash, you crack me up. Let me see a picture! Does he have tattoos too? Does he know you have them? What does he do? Is he vegetarian too? Does your family know him? What about your grandma, would she approve?" Even though we have completely contrasting lifestyles, I considered Anita a friend more than a boss and she was quite comfortable asking no less than fifty questions about the quality of guy Brian was and concluded our "bank coaching session" with "You know I'll need to meet him before I can give my approval, right?"

"If I say yes does that mean I can go home early so I can talk to him?" I joked with her. In reality, I did need to get home, and fast. I had two important calls to make that evening, and the first one wasn't going to be pleasant at all, but it needed to be made: I had to break up with the guy I had been seeing. Brian was back in my life, and there was no chance I was going to let him get away a second time. I knew what it felt like to live without him and I didn't want it to ever happen again. Once the breakup call had been made, it was time to make the second one. Brian and I spoke on the phone the rest of the night. After so many years apart, we were finally together again.

Chapter Two

"A leave chit?" I asked while giggling. Surely, he was messing with me. It sounded like a bad word, not the official Navy document Brian was trying to tell me about.

"Oh, come on, isn't there anybody you could talk to and convince to get your paperwork signed so you can come down here tomorrow?" I pleaded.

"I'm sorry, Ash, that's life in the military. I have to follow rules that people with civilian jobs don't have to think about." I could tell by the sound of his voice he didn't like letting me down, and that he was just as disappointed as I was. "And a chit is a real thing," he said, laughing.

I sighed.

"I know . . . I'm sorry! I wish I could come down there too. Each command sets their own rules as to how far a sailor can travel without taking leave, but the one I'm in now says if I leave the state I need to. I have to provide all sorts of information on it, too, so they know exactly where I am staying at, who I am going to see, relationship status to the person I am going to visit . . ." he explained, dragging out this last portion.

"Oh, really?" I said, giggling.

"Ehm, yeah . . ." I couldn't see him, but I could feel him blushing from where I was sitting.

We both laughed nervously at the mention of the word *relationship* before returning to the conversation.

"Well, I'm not going to lie, I'm bummed. It would be so fun to see you, but I understand. So how about next weekend?" I asked anxiously, already making plans for all of the fun things we could go do together if he came down. "Would that give you enough time to get your CHIT together?" I laughed far too hard at my own joke.

"Ha ha. Wow, a real zinger there, Ash. Good one." I could hear the smile in his voice. "I think so, but I'll let you know for sure once it's approved."

We spent the next week on the phone together. Talking, texting, emailing, and Facebook messaging.

January 15

9:50 p.m.

Ashley: I was reading a bunch of old journals the other night and read one where I wrote that you and I wanted to get a rottweiler together and name it Bane! Haha

9:51 p.m.

Brian: Hahaha Awesome! Wait, was that when I was in CT? Say, from around, 2004, summer-ish? We're cute.

Separated by 150 miles and a state line, we utilized every form of communication available to us, until finally, he was able to have his leave request approved. At two o'clock on Friday, January 18, 2013, he said goodbye to his coworkers, got in the car, and headed south. From the submarine port at Naval Base Kitsap in Bangor, Washington, it's pretty much a straight shot on I-5 South, and it takes about three hours to drive past the row of massive decommissioned warships sitting in dry dock in the Bremerton navy yard, through the massive Douglas fir and Sitka spruce trees lining the freeway on the outskirts of the Olympia National Forest and through various cities and towns before arriving in Portland, Oregon.

He called me as he got in his car and drove off base. "Hey, I'm on my way!"

I could hear the nervousness in his voice, and I was thankful I wasn't the only one anxiously anticipating the moment. Even my frigid downtown apartment couldn't keep me from blushing cheek to cheek as I thought of him coming to see me. I sat on my bed, nervously tapping my foot on the hardwood floors. This one-bedroom apartment had become home over the past four years I'd lived there and had everything I needed: Access to the Max light rail outside my door, a sports bar across the street that offered its patrons—and neighbors living in very close proximity—high-speed Wi-Fi (thank you, Cheerful Bullpen!), and numerous restaurants catering to my lifelong vegetarian diet within walking or biking distance. At $950 a month, the cheap rent—by downtown standards—was also an added bonus. The fact that the single-pane windows and uninsulated walls kept no heat trapped in during the cold winters didn't bother me. We could watch the Portland Timbers soccer matches from our rooftop (until they remodeled the stadium) and with my stepsister living in the apartment downstairs and never less than four or five friends occupying other apartments in the building, we bought warm jackets and kept hearty stocks of gin, whiskey, and potato vodka on our shelves. It had been a great place to live, but after talking to Brian over the past two weeks and the instant connection between us, I had a feeling that things would be changing soon and I'd potentially be trading in my city apartment for something in the suburbs, a few hours north, in the near future.

"It's on Southwest 18th and Taylor Street, right across the street from the Cheerful Bullpen bar and Timbers Stadium," I told him on the phone as he approached Portland.

"OK, great, is there parking close by?" he asked as I heard his blinker flicker on in the background. This meant he was getting close. AGHH! Brian was close! To Portland. To my apartment. To me. Brian was coming here! I couldn't believe it. He told me he needed to hang up so he could use the GPS on his phone, so we said a quick goodbye as the butterflies in my stomach came to life.

I sat down on the couch in my living room, right leg over my left one. *Nope. Change.* I got up, taking a sudden interest in my bookshelf and rearranged a few books. *Nope, too nervous to organize*. I sat back on the couch, leg jittering. Got back up. *How's my hair?* Checked myself in the mirror. *Cute*.

What if he had trouble finding somewhere to park? Between the bar and the stadium across the street, finding a parking spot was difficult, especially on a Friday night. By now, I was pacing the living room back and forth, wearing a tread into the overly painted floors and constantly checking my phone for a sign he was here.

"AGHHHHH!" I yelped as soon as I heard my phone ring—I had been holding on to it for dear life with my right hand as I marched across the room. "Heyyyy!" I answered, trying and failing miserably to sound nonchalant.

"Hey! I think I'm downstairs."

My heart was about to beat out of my chest. "OK, I'll be right down!" I opened the heavy wooden door and ran down the stairs as fast as I could before reaching the downstairs door leading to our communal patio—affectionately referred to as the stoop. My friends and I had spent endless summers on that stoop, celebrating Timbers match victories, barbecuing, talking, laughing, and having post-Sunday brunch sangria when the weather called for it. Yet, none of that mattered in this moment, because that door and that cement stoop were the only things separating me from Brian. I took a deep breath and opened the door.

Parked in front of my apartment building was a brand-new 2013 black Subaru Forester with the engine running. Brian had always had a thing for Subaru and was particularly excited and proud of this new purchase. I beamed from ear to ear at the sight of it as I ran down the cement steps connecting our stoop to the sidewalk and opened the passenger-side door.

I jumped in and we immediately embraced each other. This was the moment we had been waiting and hoping for. We eventually pulled away from each other and erupted in laughter but never breaking eye contact. We had spent nearly a decade apart, yet it felt as if we had never left each other's side. We spent the next two hours in my apartment catching up on things we hadn't covered on the phone in the weeks prior.

"What's your favorite place you've traveled to so far?" he asked, knowing I'd spent the past few years doing nothing but working and traveling around the world. "Probably South Africa. Cage diving with great white sharks was one of the greatest experiences of my life," I recalled fondly, leaving out the part about getting so seasick in the fifteen-foot waves I spent the entire boat ride home heaving over the side of the vessel.

"I loved Africa too," he exclaimed, excited to be talking about such an important time of his life. "I spent ten months there as part of a special project with the Navy, supporting the Army in Djibouti. I also got to volunteer at an orphanage in Ethiopia and spend some time in Uganda too. White-water rafting down the Nile river was one of the most exhilarating things I've ever done! I'll have to show you this picture I have of us getting dumped out of the boat! It was amazing," he recalled, a sense of pride evident in his voice and the way he spoke of these adventures. I, too, had spent some time in the water during my travels through the continent of Africa, and we sat in my cold apartment exchanging stories and catching up on the rest of our travels and the wild experiences and adventures we'd had over the years.

"When's the last time you went sailing?" he asked, knowing we shared this common passion and it was something we were excited to share with one another.

"It's been years . . . the last time I was on a sailboat was probably 2006 or 2007?" I recalled, slightly disappointed in myself realizing it had been that long. "I used to love it so much, but I've spent the past few years focusing on school, work, and travel and I don't know anybody down here who sails so it just hasn't been a part of my life for a while. I can't believe you've gotten into it though. I can't wait to go sailing with you!" I exclaimed as I invited myself on the boat I knew he had recently purchased.

"Definitely. You have to come up so we can take her out. I usually go by myself because I don't know anyone that likes sailing either, but I'd love to have you out there with me."

Minutes turned into hours and, at some point, the space heater that had been keeping us warm turned off. We had been so engrossed in conversation that neither of us noticed until I saw Brian's breath as he let out a hearty laugh. It was cold and we were hungry. We glanced at the clock, realizing it was ten p.m. and neither of us had eaten dinner. I knew Laughing Planet on NW 21th Avenue was open late and had vegan/vegetarian options to accommodate both of our diets. We grabbed our jackets and walked the twelve blocks, hand in hand, through the familiar streets of Northwest Portland. The rest of our evening was spent laughing, rekindling, and enjoying every minute we were together.

Saturday morning, we woke up wanting to do something fun and adventurous—a theme that would play out again and again throughout our relationship. We decided on hiking through the Ape Caves—one of the longest underground lava tubes in the United States of America—but once we were halfway up our drive to Mount St. Helens where they're located, we found out we couldn't access them because of the snow.

"Well, since we're already in the car, how about the coast?" I suggested.

A smile spread across Brian's face, the dimple on his left cheek making his handsome features even more pronounced, and he said, "Yes, absolutely." He turned the car around, heading south this time, and off we went, destination: the Oregon Coast. In reality, it didn't matter where we were headed. We were having so much fun together, we could have gone anywhere that day and it would have been the absolute best day ever. That being said, we'd made many memories together at the Oregon Coast in our twenties and we knew the significance of taking a trip to the coast together that Saturday morning.

"Hug Point?" he asked while looking at me from the driver's seat of his car.

"Hug Point." I smiled while responding, knowing he was choosing this location because of the time we had spent there together years before, climbing rocks and exploring the tide pools the area is known for. Two hours later, we arrived. A state park situated off Highway 101 between the towns of Cannon Beach and Manzanita, it's one of those spots you'd drive past unless you knew it was there but whose beauty is unmatched by much. After a short hike through a grove of the towering Douglas fir trees the Oregon Coast is famous for, we stepped foot on the sand. The salty smell of the Pacific Ocean and the gentle hum of the wind whipping across the waves created the perfect backdrop for this moment, and we enjoyed the rest of our afternoon together in this spot before heading back to Portland, stopping only to take a photo as the sun set on the horizon. "When is the last time you saw something so beautiful?" I asked him, in disbelief of this moment as we watched the horizon change from orange to red to blue as the sun slipped behind the clouds, eventually dipping behind the furthest stretches of ocean in front of us. "I'm looking at it right now," he responded, looking me straight in the eyes before kissing my cheek and putting his arm around me. We drove the rest of the way home holding hands and savoring our time together.

Sunday morning, we woke up to the sound of rain outside my apartment—a familiar and comfortable sound to anybody who has lived or traveled through the beautiful Pacific Northwest. Living here, you don't let the rain stop you from enjoying your day, so after making breakfast in my black-and-white-tiled kitchen, we grabbed our rain jackets and headed down the stairs, out to the stoop. We started the Subaru with no real destination in mind, eventually ending up at the Oregon Museum of Science and Industry.

Inside is an incredible multi level interactive museum, and outside, moored in the Willamette River is the USS *Blueback* submarine, a decommissioned WWII submarine open for touring and included in the cost of museum admission. While we did have a veteran—probably in his seventies—as a tour guide on the *Blueback*, Brian couldn't help pointing things out as we walked through it.

"This boat is a little different than the submarines I usually deploy on, but it's the same basic setup," he said proudly as he showed me around. "Here's where we eat," he explained as we approached the galley. "They usually make four meals a day because of the way our watch shifts are set up, but when I'm at sea, I usually only eat two or three of those."

I could tell by the look on his face he was visualizing himself in these vinyl booths on his own submarine, chowing down as quickly as possible before clearing his place to make room for the next hungry sailor. He had previously explained to me how food becomes a sense of morale while at sea, something you look forward to help break up the monotonous days of standing watch, cleaning, and sleeping before telling me, "On my last deployment, the cook onboard decided in order to increase morale he'd start adding bacon to the white rice. Once we run out of fresh fruit and veggies onboard, white rice is one of the only things I can eat that's vegetarian. The other guys on board thought it was hilarious but the joke was on them because I packed a bunch of Clif Bars in my sea bag and I ended up just eating those instead." Even with realities like these, I could feel how proud he was of his naval service, his chosen career. To be honest, I didn't really know much about his actual job or what he did on a daily basis while behind the guarded gates of his Navy base. It wasn't from lack of being interested, but with his security clearance and the nature of his job on the submarines, he simply wasn't able to tell me. I know he traveled the world and worked on different submarines, but my knowledge began and ended there.

Our weekend together was quickly coming to an end, and early Monday morning we made a quick run to Voodoo Donuts, filling one of their iconic pink boxes with vegan apple fritters and chocolate bars for his car ride home. He drove me back to my apartment in his Subaru, where we grudgingly said our goodbyes as we hugged and kissed, standing on the stoop while the cold January rain poured down on us.

"I don't want you to go," I pleaded while wrapped in his arms.

"I know, I don't want to either. This weekend was far more than I was expecting. Like I actually can't believe how amazing it was," he told me nervously. "Can you come up next weekend? We can go sailing . . . and make out? You can try to beat me in Scrabble." We both laughed at his attempt to break up the sadness we were both feeling at the thought of saying goodbye after such a perfect weekend. We eventually pulled away from each other, and I stood on the stoop watching as he walked down the steps to his black Subaru, turning around once more to blow a kiss before jumping in, putting the transmission into drive, and turning the corner toward the freeway. We spent the next month taking turns driving back and forth between Portland and Gig Harbor, talking on the phone every moment in between, making plans for the future, and unabashedly falling in love.

Jan 21, 2013

8:07 p.m.

Brian: I'm glad you distracted me. I had an epic time with you. I feel like I connect with you on a whole different level. And I really don't remember it being like this back in the day.

8:10 p.m.
Ashley: I don't think it was like this back in the day. I think we had a strong connection back then but nothing close to this. This is a pretty unique feeling for me and I'm seriously really, really excited about it. I know people aren't "supposed" to lay all of their cards out on the table when it comes to feelings and emotions but I don't have any desire to play by those rules with you. It's an odd feeling to want to be so open with someone.

As Valentine's Day approached, he made me promise him that we would always celebrate the holidays.

"No problem! We could spend the weekend on the boat? Or how about we go to the coast?" I suggested over the phone. I had done some research online and found this great little house to rent that overlooked the ocean.

I sent him the link later that night to which he said, "It's perfect!" We sent in our deposit the next day and Brian called dibs on planning the rest of the weekend.

"Hey, I'm at the store and can't decide which suit I want to buy. Can you help me?" He called me from Men's Wearhouse.

"Of course," I said, giggling.

"Alright, then I'll send you photos, so you can choose."

I received two photos soon after. *Good grief he's gorgeous!* I thought to myself as I looked at them. He looked so handsome in his new outfits: one was a black suit with a light blue tie that matched the exact shade of his eyes, and the other was a gray suit with a maroon tie.

"You're so handsome! I love them both," I texted him.

"Hmm," he wrote back. "OK I'll just get both. I want to look good for our date!"

Who buys not one, but two brand-new suits just to take me on a date for Valentine's Day? Is this guy for real? I thought while feeling weightless, a million butterflies inside of me, and a huge smile on my face.

On Valentine's Day, he took me out to dinner. The building the restaurant was in seemed very familiar to me.

"Do you remember coming here?" he asked as we pulled the car up front.

"I do, but . . ." The outside of the building had changed so much since the last time I had been there that I was having trouble piecing events together. "Wait." It finally clicked. "Is this the old Meow Meow theater!?" Vivid memories of countless hours spent in this building watching punk bands sing and sweat their hearts out came flooding in.

"Yep," he said, that dimple on his left cheek illuminated from passing cars' headlights, giving away how happy and proud he was to have been able to pull off such surprise. "It's been completely redone, and tonight it's being taken over by the Vegan Caterer for a vegan Valentine's Day dinner."

I was impressed by how much thought, effort, and love he put into planning our dinner. It was surreal. We spent the night in Portland before driving to our rented beach house in Newport, Oregon. We spent the rest of the weekend walking the beach, making love, eating vegan raspberry cheesecake, and soaking up our time together. Sunday afternoon, we started our journey home but stopped at Manzanita beach for Mexican food and to watch the sunset. We got our burritos and walked down to the beach where we took over a fire somebody had abandoned. We curled up together under a sleeping bag, holding hands, kissing, and enjoying every single moment of this intense chemistry we shared. As the sun set, however, I could sense his demeanor changing, an apprehension, and could feel his heart beating against my chest.

"What's the matter?" I asked, kissing his cheek. I knew why he was nervous. I knew what he wanted to say, but I wanted to hear it.

He took a deep breath but didn't reply. His eyes were staring at the horizon, that magical line where the sea meets the sky; a sailor on dry land, he seemed to be looking for something specific out there. Then, suddenly, he blinked, looked at me, and said in one breath: "Screw it, I'm just going to say it . . . I love you!"

Without hesitation, I curled up into his lap and whispered, "I love you too."

Chapter Three

Time and tide wait for no man. A proverb dating back to 1225, roughly translated from "And te tide and te time þat tu iboren were, schal beon iblescet" and a phrase that's become popular among those who have built their lives around the sea. Brian lived the essence of this phrase, realizing very early on that time is the most precious thing we have and just like the tides at sea, it will continue on whether you're ready or not. The fact he named his sailboat after this phrase was no less surprising than seeing these words tattooed against a colorful orange and blue shipwreck scene on his right arm. As our relationship grew, so did our connection to this phrase, and even more so our kinship to the sea. We had waited to reconnect nearly a decade, and now we were simply done waiting. We knew we wouldn't get a third chance, and this was our time.

We spent the spring of 2013 on *Time and Tide*, a 1975 Carter thirty-three-foot, three-quarter-ton sailboat. Just like Brian and me, she was a little rough around the edges, but she was ours and we couldn't get enough. With only twelve of her style in existence, she was built to Independent Offshore Racing (IOR) rule, a sloop sailboat designed to be half cruising and half racing vessel. She was hearty but fast and perfect for the two of us to spend weekends on together in the Puget Sound. *Time and Tide* was easily identified among the sea of white sailboats by her tall black mast and the line of deep blue paint running the length of her hull. At the stern of the boat was a dual cockpit fitted with a wooden tiller, which had seen high winds and offshore swells with her previous owner but was in good shape, and we both preferred this manual method of steering over the shiny wheel helms you see on most boats built today. Behind the cockpit, nestled up against the backstay, was an American flag, kept in the cabin to prevent its exposure to the elements but hoisted by hook and pulley when underway.

"How come the mainsheet traveler is set so far back?" I asked Brian as we got underway the first time he brought me sailing aboard *Time and Tide*. I'd been sailing on a handful of different sailboats, but never one quite with a setup like this with the basic controls of the rigging in the actual cockpit with us. "She's set up for racing!" he exclaimed, an excitement in his voice that indicated this was something he was interested in. "See how all of her lines and winches are set within reach of the cockpit here? This is so we can maneuver her from back here without having to go forward in dicey conditions."

"But you have roller furling!" I exclaimed, trying to impress him with my underwhelming recollection of boat terminology, but also recognizing it from the small keelboats and cruising vessels

I'd been sailing on. He smiled at me, giving away the fact he was thankful for the small luxury on the boat, something I'd soon come to be thankful for as well as we spent our weekends of the cold spring months out on the Sound, the freezing air whipping across our cheeks and three-foot wind waves causing the bow to jump up and down in the deep blue water. We'd spend our weekends huddled together in the cockpit of the boat, taking in sights of Mount Rainier and enjoying the fact we often had the entire South Puget Sound to ourselves on those cold days.

Because the previous owner had intended her to be a racing boat, the entire downstairs cabin had been gutted, except for the head—think very primitive toilet—and a wooden shelf in the V berth at the bow of the boat, which we turned into our bedroom on overnight camping adventures.

"She's not pretty," Brian had tried to warn me before I ever stepped foot on board. "The cabin needs a lot of work before I'll be completely happy, but I've been busy with work . . . and trips to Portland." He laughed.

"She's a boat! A sailboat at that, and we get to spend time together," I explained, letting him know I would have been happy in a two-person rowboat if it meant we could spend our time together out on the water. It only took one night on *Time and Tide* for it to quickly become a way of life for us. That first night, we slept huddled between two sleeping bags we'd zipped together, on the hard, wooden shelf suspended in the V berth. The sound of waves gently crashing against her hull and the smell of fresh ocean air—we couldn't have cared less where we were, only that we were together, but the fact that we both found it to be the most romantic moment we'd ever been a part of was truly icing on the cake.

"Babe, this is unreal. This is so cool!" we kept saying to one another. We were in love with each other but also with these moments we were experiencing together. On the water, on a sailboat, and with each other; there was truly no other place either of us wanted to be. Brian eventually went to the local fabric store and purchased six-inch-thick bright green upholstery foam to make our sleeping accommodations a little more comfortable, but truthfully, we slept very little while out on our weekends on *Time and Tide*, instead enjoying our time together wrapped in each other's arms, playing cribbage, and daydreaming about the places we'd take her. In addition to the foam padding, we brought aboard a single-burner propane camping stove Brian found at an REI sample sale.

"Guess how much this was?" he asked me with a giant smile on his face, obviously proud of his purchase.

"Hmm . . . $100?" I teased him, knowing how excited he was to be showing me this great deal of a camping stove.

"Fourteen dollars!" he exclaimed. "Can you believe it? I should have bought two!"

We used that camping stove to make meals ranging from gourmet veggie burgers to Top Ramen, but mostly for heating endless amounts of hot water in order to fill our French press with the strong coffee the Pacific Northwest is known for being home to. Hot coffee has never tasted as good as it does fresh out of a French press while sailing through Colvos Passage in the South Puget Sound. I'd drink my coffee while seated in the companionway of *Time and Tide*, watching Brian tighten the sail trim and tidy lines, keenly unaware of how handsome he was in these moments. A sailor at sea and the captain of his boat, I'd pass his black coffee back to him, and he'd drink it with gloved hands while looking up at the wind indicator or watching the red and green telltales looking for subtle shifts in the wind. From the companionway, I couldn't help but fall deeper and further in love with him and these moments we were sharing together.

On weekends when Brian couldn't come to Portland, I would drive up to visit him in Gig Harbor, and soon enough we didn't even have to make plans—it was just assumed we'd be spending the weekend out on the water, sailing *Time and Tide*. In the beginning, we moored her at Peninsula Yacht Basin (PYB), a marina less than two miles from Brian's house at the bottom of Peacock Hill. Driving down Peacock Hill toward PYB is an experience of its own as you're confronted with sweeping views of the harbor—filled year-round with boats from all over the Pacific Northwest docking up at Tides Tavern for a quick pint or finding shelter among the fleet of fishing vessels Gig Harbor was put on the map for. You also get views of Mount Rainier to the east, the iconic Tacoma Narrows Bridge to the south, and in the warm summer months you can catch the Gig Harbor junior sailing club racing back and forth between buoy markers. The PYB marina is a well-known landmark in this charming coastal town, perched at the end of a long dock made of railroad-tie-looking planks, which jet out over the water. As the tide comes and goes throughout the day, the dock ladder leading to our slip would rise and lower, exposing a tide pool underneath the marina office.

"Babe! Look at this starfish! It's massive!" he'd exclaim if he was the first one down the ramp.

"Look at this one! I've never seen a purple one like this before," I'd point out as we went back and forth marveling at the variety of starfish, sea anemones, and other sea life living on these pilings, unbeknownst to anyone who didn't take the time to look. We loved feeling like we were connecting to these stunning sea creatures and, the more we sailed, the wilder our experiences became. Once, after a particularly fun weekend exploring McMicken Island, we were motoring back toward the Tacoma Narrows Bridge when we came upon a fleet of five boats stopped in the water at various points across the channel. Picking up the VHF radio, we overheard, "Orcas! North. Northwest." Brian looked at me, I looked at him, and he pulled the radio closer to his ear as he cut the engine and we scrambled from the stern to the bow in a matter of moments, gripping the starboard shrouds and balancing ourselves on the deck, searching the water for any sight of black and white. He saw them first.

"ASH! Look!" he yelled into the wind as he held my hand, squeezing it with excitement.

We couldn't believe our eyes. Four, five, maybe six orca whales, all gliding effortlessly through the fast-moving channel, headed north and under the bridge—the same direction we'd been headed moments before. We stood on the deck of *Time and Tide* watching these beautiful creatures for as long as we could see them. When they were out of sight, we started the engine back up and followed their path as we made way into our home port of Gig Harbor, both in shock we had just seen a pod of orcas in our backyard, from our sailboat.

"Did that really just happen?" We exchanged words and looks of disbelief with each other.

"Orcas!? Seriously, whose life is this?! I've been out here a hundred times and I've never seen anything like that," Brian said while shaking his head, amazed at the chance encounter. This was just one more reason we knew we were special together, and getting to experience moments like these together was something neither of us would ever forget.

By the end of spring, we'd had several more encounters with the resident sea creatures living beneath the waters of the Puget

Sound, including a variety of seals, sea lions, Dall's porpoises, and eventually even an encounter with the rarely seen harbor porpoise. We were under sail one afternoon on our way up to Seattle; the only sound onboard was the faint hum of wind hitting our mainsail at the perfect angle. The wind was steady so we had the autohelm steering the boat for us while Brian and I were sitting next to each other on the port side rail heavily immersed in a competitive game of cribbage.

Tap. Tap.

"Did you hear that?" Brian asked, strengthening his back as if the newly assumed position would help him hear better.

"Hear what?" I sat up straight, too, trying to mimic him.

Tap. Tap.

"That!" he exclaimed. This time, I had heard it too.

Tap. Tap.

"What is that?" We both looked around in an attempt to locate what or who was causing the tapping against the hull of *Time and Tide*.

Brian went forward before looking back at me, a look of bewilderment across his face. I joined him on the deck and that's where we saw them: harbor porpoises! We stood together, not believing our eyes as these two porpoises played in the water mere feet away from us, riding our bow wave, and letting us watch them. Brian's eyes were wide open with surprise, his lips moving as if trying to express the joy he was feeling but words failed him, so he just kept glancing at me, squeezing my hand, and then returning his gaze to the porpoises, who looked like they were happy we had finally noticed them. After our chance encounter with the orca whales a few weeks prior, we didn't think anything was going to top that. However, once again we found ourselves exaggeratedly saying,

"Did that just happen!?" and we embraced and sealed the moment with a passionate kiss. There was a childlike quality to Brian's reaction, an innocence usually lost in men who've experienced the world the way Brian had. I didn't know it was possible, but I fell even more in love with him in that moment. As the porpoises began swimming away from us, Brian exploded in a hearty laughter, saying, "You must be good luck!" revealing how special and surreal that encounter had been for him. I still stood there, taking it all in. *Don't ever forget this moment, Ash.* I reminded myself.

Later that spring, the Bremerton City Marina had a slip open up and we decided to move *Time and Tide* for a change of scenery. Being moored there would enable us to explore different areas of the Puget Sound than we'd had access to while at PYB. Twenty minutes north of Gig Harbor, we'd drive up to the marina and venture out on Friday-night sunset cruises, cuddled up together on the bow, watching the sunset change the colors covering Mount Rainier. We would use the power of her sails to explore the islands scattered around the Sound, dropping anchor and kayaking through the gentle waves in the red and blue sea kayaks we'd purchased on a whim from our local harbor store. One of our favorite things to do during our weekends aboard *Time and Tide* was to grab a mooring ball in Blakely Harbor, a protected little cove on the other side of Blake Island in front of Seattle. From there, we could enjoy the sights of the Seattle skyline (including post-Mariners game fireworks!), always falling asleep with the waves gently rocking the boat, the sound of the salty seawater lapping at her hull. When the weekend would come to an end, we would drive home enjoying memories of holding hands while reading, watching movies on our shared iPad, or slow dancing in the galley, whispering to each other how incredible it was that weekends spent like this had become our new normal.

"I know we've only been dating a few months, but it's hard to imagine life before this now," I said to Brian on a particularly romantic weekend on the boat.

"I know . . . honestly, I didn't know I could be this happy. I didn't think anybody out there would love this stuff as much as I do, and I can't believe that it's you!"

"Are you kidding me? The ocean, adventure, a sailboat, and a hot captain? What's not to love?" I teased.

Brian's love of the ocean and all things water-related was contagious as days and nights at sea became our thing. Brian was the Captain, I was his First Mate, and *Time and Tide* was our home away from home. We felt at peace out on the water, in our element, but constantly aware of the potential for danger and excitement.

Brian's love of the sea translated well to his career, and he'd recently been promoted to a special projects team in the Navy called Detachment Unmanned Underwater Vehicles (Det UUV), a subdivision of Submarine Development Squadron Five (Comsubdevron 5). Of course, this was all a foreign language when he explained it to me, however I did quickly find out this meant he'd be traveling a lot. We did our best to stay in constant communication via our newly shared Verizon family plan, and he'd find ways to make sure we stayed connected, even when apart. Before leaving on any trip, he'd leave me with his gray USS *Ohio* submarine sweatshirt—a submarine he'd previously been attached to—saying, "I'm always coming back home to you, Ash. I know it's not the same, but I wore this sweatshirt every night for six months on my last deployment, so just think of it as being in my arms until we're back together and can enjoy the real thing." That sweatshirt soon became mine, and to this day it is one of my most prized possessions.

The traveling back and forth across states quickly became more and more tedious for the both of us, and we didn't like having to go five days in the middle of the week without seeing each other, so one day while on the phone, we came up with a plan.

"Hey babe, I've got a crazy schedule these next couple of weeks," Brian started off the long-distance phone conversation with.

"OK . . . how crazy? Can we still spend next weekend together?"

"I just had a last-minute work trip come up so now I'm going to be gone all next week. I'll be home for twenty-four hours but then fly out again, so it might be a couple of weeks before I can come back down to see you."

"What! No!" I pouted on the other end of the phone.

"I know, babe, I'm sorry. We can plan something for when I'm back?" he tried, knowing I was disappointed.

"OK, wait, you'll be home for twenty-four hours between trips? What if we get together then? What if we meet in the middle somewhere so that neither of us have to drive the three hours? Even if it's just for a few hours?" I asked, thinking out loud more than actually planning it out.

"Aw, babe, I don't want to go that long without seeing you either. OK, yes, let's do that!" he responded, as I let those words sink in.

While on the phone, we looked at a map of the Interstate 5 corridor and pointed to the spot in the middle of our two homes: Chehalis, Washington. Famous for its Veterans Memorial Museum, Chehalis-Centralia Railroad, and maximum-security juvenile prison Green Hill, which—ironically—I'd happened to volunteer at during my college years. Short on time, we looked up hotels in Chehalis and were directed to the charming Relax Inn, conveniently located directly across the street from the prison. After all, nothing says romance like spending a night with the love of your life in a prison parking lot motel! Nevertheless, we were hopelessly in love and just wanted to be together, so two weeks later, in between flights for Brian and right after work for me, we each drove ninety minutes—headed toward each other—and spent the night together at this off-the-beaten-path motel. We got a few questioning side glances from the eighty-year-old woman behind the yellow Formica desk while checking us in that Tuesday afternoon, but we couldn't have cared less. We took our key and walked to our room, laughing hysterically the entire way about how ridiculous yet amazing this adventure felt.

As delightful as it was to wake up to prison floodlights filling the $89-a-night hotel room, after our second midweek rendezvous at the Relax Inn, we decided it was time to make the leap and start talking about moving to the same city. Brian couldn't move to Portland because of his career in the Navy, so that meant I would be moving to Gig Harbor. I was madly in love with Brian, but this move would mean I would have to quit my job at the bank and pack up the life I'd made for myself in Portland in order to be with him. And because of the nature of his job, being with him meant spending a lot of time apart.

This was my first introduction to my life as a future military spouse: Brian's job would have to come before anything and anyone, including me. When the Navy called, he had to answer, and sometimes that meant he'd be getting out of bed and headed into work in the middle of the night because of an emergency. There was also the fact that because of the secrecy that surrounded his job, there was very little information he could share with me regarding his whereabouts, how long he would have to be gone for, and what he would be doing while away from me. Being a Navy spouse was a whole new territory for me. The terminology was different, deployments were different, and since Brian mostly worked on submarines, he would be out of reach for months at a time, until all of a sudden he would pop up somewhere in the world and my phone would ring, displaying a number I didn't recognize, with him on the other end saying, "Hey, babe! I'm in Greece!"

Even though moving to Gig Harbor would be a big change, I was incredibly excited to finally move in with Brian and have the opportunity to live under the same roof. I had envisioned Brian and me coming home after work, the two of us slow dancing in the kitchen while our dinner burned on the stove, laughing together while sitting on the couch watching our favorite TV shows, photos of the two of us together decorating the walls and the fridge, and so many other mundane events that, put together, make a house a home, and turn a couple into a family.

I also took a lot of pride in supporting Brian and his career. Brian had worked very hard in order to get where he was and, as I began the process of moving up to Gig Harbor, he told me he'd "made board" to be looked at for a promotion to Chief Petty Officer. This would take him from an E6 to an E7, meaning the seventh enlisted rank in the United States Navy, a promotion that had been authorized by the US Congress in 1920 for the first time. He would eventually fulfill his dream a few months later, in an elegant and dignified ceremony held at the Bangor Plaza on Naval Base Kitsap in Silverdale, Washington. This was Brian's accomplishment, but his closest friends and family all beamed with pride as he was pinned. Chief Petty Officer Bugge never looked more handsome.

Chapter Four

Mon Eve - 9/9

Dear Brian,

I am not much for talking on "Ma Bell" as my hearing isn't that good; but Ashley mentioned that you have an award coming up and just wanted to say "Congratulations!" I can think of happy times and events, but I don't think I would enjoy going down to deeper ends of the Ocean. I know our submarines are beautifully built and very safe, but I think I would enjoy the Cruise Ships—I'm glad I went on various cruises when I did with my sisters—it was when I was living and enjoying the "fast lane". I really *enjoyed*. It sounds like you and my lovely Ashley have a lot in common. I receive beautiful cards and letters from her, telling me all the fun things you do. So again congratulations to you Brian

> and I am so looking forward to meeting you someday!!! Don't get old, *just enjoy*! But remember, Ashley is very precious to me.

"Babe, isn't this your grandma's handwriting?" Brian asked while showing me an envelope he'd just pulled from the mailbox.

My grandmother Isabel had very distinctive writing, which Brian had seen a number of times in the handwritten letters I received from her every few weeks. I recognized it the instant I saw it, and apparently Brian did, too, as he showed me that it had been addressed to him.

"It is! She wrote you a letter!?" I exclaimed, touched that one of the most important people in my life would make the effort to do this, and a little curious as to what she had written him.

He had heard a lot about my grandma, whose life motto had always been *Just Enjoy!* As far as I can remember, she had always lived these words and ingrained it in our heads. She had nine grandchildren—she and my grandfather had had three girls and each of the three girls had had three children. Yet, she had a unique way of making each one of us feel extra special to her. She'd invite all nine grandchildren to her and my grandpa's three-bedroom house in the small coastal town of Tiburon, located just over the Golden Gate Bridge in Marin County, San Francisco, California, where we'd spend two weeks of every summer, somehow all fitting in those tiny bedrooms, or camped out in the basement floor where we'd use their built-in bar to play "Cheers!" and greet my brother "NORM!" as he walked down the stairs.

Summers spent with our grandmother always had a magical feel to them, and I loved telling Brian stories of how my grandma made me feel special, loved, and supported in everything I wanted to do. I'd call Grandma Isabel to tell her about something exciting happening in my life, or a trip I had planned somewhere, and she'd encourage me, saying, "That's great, Ash! Honey, just enjoy! But don't get old, it's the pits."

It takes a special person to make you feel confident, capable, strong, and secure in the fact that you are loved unconditionally. Brian made me feel the same way, albeit in a slightly different context.

Brian knew how important my grandma was to me, which by default made her important to him as well. They hadn't met yet, but they were now pen pals and two of my biggest supporters. A few weeks after this letter arrived, I was on the phone with my grandma, telling her about a trip my mom and I had just booked to Peru and Bolivia.

"Hi, Grandma, it's Ashley!"

"Zachary?"

"Ashley. It's Ashley!" I said, a little louder this time, picturing her petite, white-haired frame standing in her kitchen, squinting her bright blue eyes at the cordless phone in her hand, trying to figure out which of her nine grandkids was calling her.

"A–SH–LEYYY," I said again, louder and slower to give her a chance to hear it.

"Oh, Ashley? Hi, sweetheart! I couldn't hear you through this stupid phone. How are you?"

"I'm good! Just calling to say hi," I began before eventually asking her, "Did mom tell you that we're going to South America?"

"She did! Oh, Ash, I think that's just so wonderful you're doing all of this traveling with your mother. I loved seeing your pictures from Russia earlier this year, I can't wait to hear all about Peru and Bolivia." My grandma was always incredibly supportive of my adventures, always encouraging those around her to live their lives and not take one moment for granted, always finding a way to work in her catchphrase, “Honey, Just Enjoy!”

A few weeks later, Brian and I said our goodbyes before he flew to Washington, DC, for a work trip and I met up with my mom to begin our adventure to South America. Our itinerary would be aggressive as we wanted to see as much of the two countries as possible during our two-week visit. Our itinerary included visiting the cities of Lima, Chivay, Puno, Cusco, and concluding in Aquas Calientes—a beautiful, picturesque little town situated at the bottom of the mountain where Machu Picchu is. It is surrounded by a green valley with waterfalls and a river running through the town. After my mom and I placed our luggage in our hotel room, we ventured out to the open-air market, just down the hill from our hotel. The market was filled with Peruvian venders and all of their trinkets for sale: picture frames, clocks, and bright hand-woven clothing as far as the eye could see; walking through would be a fun way to spend our first afternoon in town.

“Ash, he wants fifteen sol for these shirts, is that a good deal? How much is that?” she asked as I stood there offering apologetic eyes to the vendor.

“Yes, mom, that’s a good deal—it’s like five bucks,” I said quickly, trying to get her to pay so I didn’t have to watch her barter anymore. I’ve never liked bargaining and I especially didn’t want to be in the middle of this intense T-shirt negotiation going on. I took a step back and walked on to the next booth waiting for my mom who eventually appeared, feeling triumphant for talking the vendor down to fourteen sol for the shirts.

We walked back to the hotel to unload our souvenirs and so I could check my phone and see if Brian had messaged me. It was hard being away from him, even when on great adventures in foreign countries. I missed him. We'd had very spotty cell phone reception during our travels the past two weeks and between that and the time difference, we were sending and receiving messages at all hours of the day, but the messages were always sweet:

"Babe! I miss you so much. Have so much fun today, I can't wait to see pictures. Eight more days!"

"Hey! Things are great here but I can't wait to be back home with you. I miss your lips. Five more days!"

"Are you home yet!? The house is so lonely without you here. I'm so glad you're having fun, but hurry home!"

Once in our room, my mom got in the shower while I started putting my souvenirs in my suitcase. I grabbed my phone off the charger and saw that Brian had tried to FaceTime me multiple times. *I know he misses me, but that's strange,* I thought, a sense of dread suddenly coming over me. I tried FaceTiming him back but he didn't answer. *What in the world?* I started getting a pit in my stomach. I clicked out of the FaceTime app and found a handful of text messages from my Aunt Sharon, my mother's sister, urging me to call her as soon as possible. *Oh no!! What is happening? Brian? One of my brothers? What is going on and why isn't Brian answering his phone?* Meanwhile, my mom was in the shower and I was beginning to panic so I messaged my Aunt Sharon back.

"Aunt Sharon! We just got back to our room. Brian tried to FaceTime me but I wasn't here. What's going on?"

"Ash, I'm so sorry to do this while you guys are in Peru, but Grandma is in the hospital, with stage IV heart failure." She texted back quickly, "It's not looking good, and I think you should call if you can. Cousin Jen and Aunt DeeDee are with her now."

Grandma?! In the hospital? Heart failure? What? I felt as if a ton of bricks had just crashed onto me. I sat down on my bed, barely holding my phone with both hands. I could feel my eyes welling up in tears, my lower lip quivering. I heard the water in the shower slowing its flow, an indication that my mom was just about done and was close to stepping into the bedroom. I was about to tell her that my grandma—her mother—was in the hospital and they were saying it's not looking good and we were in the middle of the jungle in Peru. I slowly turned my head toward the bathroom door as it opened, looked at my mother whose smile drained from her face as she asked me, "Ashley! What's wrong?" She saw the look on my face as she came out of the bathroom, but her tone implied she had no idea what I was about to tell her.

"Mom! It's grandma . . ." Words barely made it out of my throat. "She's in the hospital . . ."

My mom walked closer to me, eyes wide open, her chin slightly tilted to the side, not understanding where I was going with this.

"Mom," I cried, "Aunt Sharon says she's in heart failure and she's not gonna make it." Tears started falling down my cheeks. I couldn't control them.

"What!?" my mom gasped. "What are you talking about?"

"Aunt Deedee and Jen are with grandma and we need to find a way to call them right now." My mom came and sat on the bed, wrapped in her towel, hair still dripping wet from her shower. She sat next to me and we tried to digest this news together as I feverishly messaged my Aunt Sharon for information.

As I was messaging her, my phone sprang to life. It was Brian! Finally, he was FaceTiming me back.

"Ash, I'm so sorry," he began as soon as he picked up the phone.

"Brian, what's happening? Aunt Sharon isn't writing me back and I can't make any calls from this phone. What's going on?" I begged, hoping he would tell me everything was going to be OK.

He told me he had talked to my Aunt Sharon and that my grandma had gotten very sick very quickly and had been taken to the hospital where they found she was in stage IV heart failure and wasn't going to survive. He knew my grandma was one of my best friends in the world and the words he was delivering to me were going to be excruciating to receive. He told me he had already begun planning our return to San Francisco, but because we had at least a two-day trip ahead of us, first by bus, then train, and the flight out of Peru, in all honesty we probably wouldn't make it to San Francisco in time to say goodbye to her.

"Babe, I just can't . . . it's my grandma . . ." I cried into the phone with him.

"I know, sweetheart. I know. Listen, I'm trying to get you home as soon as possible, OK? Tell me what you want to do."

"I don't know . . . I just can't believe it. I just need to talk to her."

"Can you go downstairs and ask someone in the hotel lobby if they have a phone you can use to call the States? Somebody might let you and you could talk to her?" I was incredibly touched by how much he cared about me being able to say goodbye to my grandmother, and by how much effort he had put into planning our trip back home. After getting as many details from him as possible, I rushed down to the reception and tried, in my very broken Spanish, to ask the receptionist if I could use his phone to make a call to the United States.

"Por favor, señor," I began, stuttering. "I need . . . yo quiero . . . no, necesito el phone, please!" As I tried to gesture a phone with my right hand, placing my thumb by my ear and the pinky by my mouth, I held out all the cash I had on me at the time and thankfully he understood and, in a broken English, offered me his personal cell phone so I could make the call. I rushed back up to my room and with trembling fingers I dialed my cousin's phone number.

I started crying as soon as she picked up. "Jennifer, I talked to Brian, what's going on?"

"I'm so sorry, Ashley, it doesn't make any sense." Jennifer could barely pronounce these words before breaking down and crying along with me.

"But how is this possible? She's so healthy, she wasn't even sick, this can't be happening!" I begged, pleaded, in the hopes that this would somehow change what was about to happen.

"I know, Ash," was all my cousin was able to say.

"Can I talk to her? I can be there in two days, Jennifer, just two days. Please just tell her she needs to hold on for two days—"

I noticed my mother walking behind me, but what I hadn't realized was that I had actually stepped outside of our room and was now walking up and down the hall, speaking loudly in English.

"I have to talk to her, please . . ." I told my cousin.

"Hi, Ash, it's Grandma. Please don't be sad." I was crying so hard I could barely catch my breath. "Oh, sweetheart, there is no reason to cry. I'm going home and I'm going to see Grandpa!"

"Grandma, I'm coming there, OK?" I reassured her, but I then realized she didn't need to be reassured. In fact, she started singing "So Long, Farewell," which had been a favorite song of hers since we were young children watching *The Sound of Music* during our summers with her.

"Brian is going to be there, too, so please just wait, I'll be there soon."

She sounded content. She wasn't scared, she wasn't sad, she was firm in her Catholic beliefs and knew what was waiting for her when she closed her eyes.

"Grandma, you have to hang on, OK?"

"Honey, don't you worry about me. I'll be fine, I know where I'm going . . ."

I couldn't stop crying. I was wiping my tears on my T-shirt, still walking up and down the hall.

"I love you, honey, you've always been so special to me, Ash."

My grandmother, Isabel Ann Maxson, passed away on October 13, 2013.

The flight home from Peru was one of the longest of my life. It took over thirty-six hours, as I flew into Portland with my mom and drove the three hours home to Gig Harbor where Brian met me, wrapping his arms around me the instant we saw each other. I knew my grandmother's faith was strong and she was resolved in the idea of where she'd be going after taking her last breath, but I was devastated by the fact she had passed away before I had even had the chance to introduce her in person to Brian. A few days later, we packed our bags and headed to the airport, this time bound for San Francisco where Brian would meet the rest of my family for the very first time.

All my cousins had arrived in San Francisco for our grandmother's funeral, and with minimal coordination, we all decided there was no place we'd rather be than at our grandma's house, just as we did during those summers of our childhood. When I explained to Brian our sleeping arrangements, his eyes became wide and he raised his eyebrows in a way that conveyed he was certainly not expecting to have to sleep on the living room floor with me and all of my grown cousins. And their spouses. And their kids. But he was a trooper and knew it was important to me, so he did it anyway. I was anxious for my entire family to get to know this man I'd been telling them all about; however, this was certainly not the way I had planned on going about making it happen.

We arrived in San Francisco around ten p.m., rented a car, and drove the hour to my grandma's house. By the time we arrived it was dark and almost everyone was asleep. My Aunt Sharon had laid bedding out for us on the desk by the door and we tiptoed through the entryway, stepping over my cousin Tyler, his wife Kira, and their two children in search of an open space on the floor. We eventually found one, between my little brother, Ben, and another cousin, Beau. Perfect. We'd be cozy, but we'd all be together. Early the next morning as we woke up, a bit sore from the hard floor, we heard noise coming from the kitchen: ice cubes clinking together, a blender, laughter, and the catchphrase we'd all come to know and love, "Just Enjoy!" I didn't have to see it to know what was going on in the kitchen; instead, I turned to Brian and asked him if he wanted a gin fizz for breakfast.

"A gin fizz?" Brian looked puzzled. "Babe, it's like seven in the morning."

I smiled. Brian was new to this family, but he'd soon learn it just wouldn't be a trip to my grandma's house without the delectable combination of gin, lemonade concentrate, half and half, and ice twirled together until smooth in the blender and served out of a Lake Placid ice-skating glass from her wooden wine glass holder. This was tradition.

"Trust me," I said coyly as we stood up, shook ourselves off, and stepped over the rest of my cousins still sleeping on the floor to greet the party already forming in the kitchen.

After breakfast, we all took turns between the two bathrooms in grandma's house, getting ready to head out for the day. It didn't take much discussion to decide what we'd be doing that day to honor my grandma as a family. We divided ourselves between all of the rental cars and crossed the Golden Gate Bridge into the city, headed for the intersection of Hyde and Beach streets and the Buena Vista Cafe. We grew up going to this cafe, the nine cousins all taking turns waiting in line across the street for the cable cars while my grandma, mom, and aunts enjoyed Irish coffees at the often-standing-room-only cafe. Grandma Isabel would order one and then another, just enjoying, until she said she felt "glowy," at which time she'd ask for the bill, always treating everyone she was with, and telling everyone younger than her, "Honey, let me treat. This is how I enjoy my money; someday you'll have kids and grandkids, and you can do the same."

We were a group of twenty-four people who somehow all managed to get two giant round tables together, and we all smiled as the familiar sight of Irish coffee and large breakfast platters appeared in front of us. We ate, drank, and laughed as the older cousins sent their kids across the street to wait in line for the cable cars just as we had done when we were the same age. We recounted stories of "And do you remember that time when grandma . . ." and "Oh my gosh, how about when . . ." Brian sat next to me in the chair by the window, holding my hand tightly, watching me as I laughed along with the rest of my family, taking his turn to laugh at the ridiculous antics as well, getting to know her through our stories, and being surprised at our attitude toward her passing: We weren't there to mourn; rather, we were there to celebrate her life. We spent well over two hours at the café, just enjoying our time there, and racking up a hefty tab to go with it.

At one point, as the laughter started to die down, Brian excused himself to the restroom. I watched him walk away, cousin Peter quickly recalling my attention by telling yet another story, this time regarding how grumpy my grandpa was. Soon after, the waiter came by and my mom and two aunts asked for the bill.

"Oh, no need for the bill, ma'am," explained the waiter. "That gentleman already took care of it." And he pointed at Brian, who had worked his way through the crowd and just reclaimed his spot next to me.

I placed my other hand in front of my slightly opened mouth and gawked at him. I was so surprised by his gesture that all I could do was whisper, "Babe!" and reached for his hand to say thank you.

I was wrapped up in the moment, looking at Brian and thinking of what an incredibly sweet gesture he had just made for my entire family when I heard it.

"What! No! Brian, no!" came in unison from my grandma's three daughters sitting together at the other table.

I looked over to see their faces all looking very stern, like somebody had just told an inappropriate joke at the dinner table instead of the kind gesture of paying our $500 bar tab. I glanced at Brian who, obviously confused about what was happening with their reaction, glanced at me to say, "Huh?"

He squeezed my hand and squirmed a little in his seat, quite uncomfortable with the shift in dynamic and unexpected reaction as he furrowed his brow toward them to again say, "Excuse me?"

My Aunt Sharon took charge of the conversation. "Brian, NO! You're not paying!" Brian glanced at me, eyes wide open as if to telepathically ask me, *Oh crap! What just happened? Did I do something wrong?*

The proud smile he'd walked back to our table with slowly drained from his face. As the newest member of this extended family, he wasn't aware of the unspoken family rule that the oldest pays for everything and, being that my mom and her two sisters had possession of grandma's American Express card, grandma was still considered the oldest and would be posthumously treating us all to these final Irish coffees in her honor.

"I'm . . . I'm sorry?" he said in a questioning tone, as if to double-check he had actually done something he needed to apologize for.

My mother walked with purpose toward the cash register, leaned closer to the waiter, who checked the bill and whispered, "It's $500, ma'am."

"Thank you," she replied in a firm tone.

Seated back at the table, she got my grandma's checkbook out of her purse, scribbled something on it, and then gave it to Brian, who stared at it long enough as if to make sure this was indeed happening. My mother and her sisters were shaking their heads as Brian sat there incredibly uncomfortable with the interaction, still trying to process what had just happened when Aunt Sharon said, "Grandma would have wanted to treat so that we could all just enjoy!"

Brian talked about that interaction the entire drive home. He laughed it off but had to ask again and again if that had really just happened, if he had really been scolded by the three new reigning matriarchs of my family. I kissed his hand and assured him that yes, it had and yes, he had—but it really was what my grandma would have wanted. We pulled up to a stoplight on the corners of Van Ness and Lombard, heading back toward the bridge, when he squeezed my hand, looked over at me and said, "If we ever have a daughter, I think we should name her Isabel after your grandma."

I was speechless. We had recently moved in together—a huge step for a young couple, and no matter how committed we were to each other, we had taken that step quickly in our relationship—but now this man was talking about making babies with me? I had to take a deep breath to make sure we really were having this conversation. My grandmother meant so much to me, and her spirit and way of life had always breathed a sense of adventure and wonder in me; to hear Brian say that he wanted our daughter—if we ever had one—to be named after her meant the world to me, because it showed me he understood and actually *felt* how much my grandma meant to me and what she represented in my life. I stared at Brian with tears in my eyes, my lower lip quivering, overcome with emotion from the weekend and now of this moment. He smiled at me as the light turned green and resumed driving. We held hands, each deep in thought of what this conversation meant to us as individuals and as a couple while we drove toward the Golden Gate Bridge, back into Marin County, and toward the festivities and slumber party awaiting us at my grandma's house.

We spent the next few days with my family, celebrating Grandma Isabel's life and enjoying our time with each other before Brian and I left my grandma's and drove into San Francisco in order to spend our last night in town together. We checked into our hotel and walked around Fisherman's Wharf, Pier 39, and Ghirardelli Square as I recounted stories of my childhood and countless times spent in those exact places with my grandma. Eventually, my brother Zack texted me that he and my cousin Peter were headed into the city and we spent the rest of the evening with them, drinking, laughing, and cheering to Grandma.

Things between Brian and me changed once we returned to Gig Harbor. We had just been through tragedy and heartache together, the loss of a loved one, then a talk about what to name our future daughter, if we ever had one. We were desperately in love with one another. So much so that we were both crushed when he came home from work a few days later to tell me he'd had orders come through and he'd be deploying in the next few weeks.

Chapter Five

"Hey babe," Brian said, looking at me with a concerned look. "We need to talk. I know we've done a few weeks apart here and there with my work travel, but this is going to be a full deployment. We need to talk through this a little and put some plans in place, OK?"

"What do you mean, full deployment? Where are you going? How long will you be gone? Will we get to talk? Can I come meet you somewhere? Can I send you care packages? But I'm going to miss you!" I blurted out every thought in my head as it came to me. He'd had nine years of getting used to this, but I was new to this military life and I hadn't been through a full deployment before with him.

There were very few answers he could actually provide me at the time, but soon I would find out he'd be joining the USS *San*

Juan, a submarine currently in port in Dubai. We knew this would be a solid six-month deployment, and our first time as a couple being away from each other for this long of a stretch. Brian would be living underwater, with at least 180 other men, working in a submarine with no windows nor internet, not even the luxury of his own bed.

"What do you mean you're sharing a bed with someone!?" I asked, trying to get a clear picture in my mind of my six-foot-two Brian cuddled up next to another sailor in one of those tiny berths.

"Ha ha, get your mind out of the gutter, babe." He laughed. "It's called hot racking. Basically, I get the rack for twelve hours to sleep, use my computer, read, whatever else, and then I move my stuff over and the other guy uses the same bunk while I work for the next twelve hours. We just trade back and forth so we're never in it together. We do this the entire time we're at sea, until I come home to you!"

While he couldn't tell me much about what he did, I loved hearing stories like these from Brian. They were so far away from anything I'd ever experienced before, and knowing he did this not only for his job but as a service to his country gave me a sense of pride in my man for all that he was and all that he aspired to be. Deployments might break some couples, but they would not break us.

With our weekends together quickly coming to a close before he left on deployment, on Saturday, November 9, we set out for an overnight sailing trip on *Time and Tide* to our favorite mooring spot: Blakely Harbor. As Brian expertly maneuvered his way out of our slip at the Bremerton marina, we motored past the East-bound Seattle/Bremerton Ferry, a commuter ferry offering drive-on service from Bremerton to Seattle and granting sweeping views of Seattle and the surrounding Puget Sound. Once we'd made it into the channel and had cleared the bend past Wautauga Beach, he leaned forward to give me a kiss and I could tell he was suddenly getting nervous. He stood up and sat down, looking around us, glancing from the wind indicator at the top of the mast and then over to me, moving his fingers and jittering his leg. I knew him well enough to know he was up to something.

"Babe," I whispered, "what's up, are you OK?"

He looked at me, smiled, and said: "Do you know how much I love you?"

I nodded, turning my head slightly to show him I was interested to see where this was going.

"I'm so thankful you came back into my life. Ashley, you've always pushed me to be a better version of myself. You give me the confidence to do things I've always dreamed of doing but never actually did. Things I didn't know I was capable of doing, I've been able to do because of your support. You are the most beautiful person I've ever met and I'm so unbelievably thankful for you. I love you. I hope you know how much I love you."

Brian had always been the sweetest boy I'd ever known, so it wasn't unusual for him to say these types of things. What was unusual was the fact that as he was saying them, I put my hands around his face, and I could feel his pulse growing by the second as he was a bundle of nerves.

"Babe! Ha ha, why are you being a freak?" I prodded him with a grin on my face.

He looked at me, laughed, and asked: "What could possibly make the weekend any better?"

"Hot chocolate?" I teased, starting to get an idea of where he might be headed with these thoughts.

He smiled at me before reaching into his pocket. He pulled out a stunning engagement ring, got down on one knee—as much as he could in the cockpit of our sailboat—and asked me to be his wife. I screamed. It was probably forty degrees out, November in the Pacific Northwest, the wind was blowing; I had gloves, sweatshirts, a jacket, and a red wool hat on; but I screamed and wrapped my arms around his neck as we both laughed, cried, and embraced one another. Up to that day, it was hands down the happiest moment of my entire life.

Deciding where to get married took all of two seconds. There was no question that we would be married in Manzanita, Oregon. The spot where we had exchanged our first "I love you" months before and the place where we looked forward to a lifetime of happy moments as we built our lives and our family together. The *when* was a little trickier. He proposed on a Saturday and we wanted to spend our weekend camping on the boat and kayaking around Blake Island State Park, celebrating our engagement before heading back to our slip Sunday afternoon. Monday was Veterans Day, so we both had it off work and could spend the day shopping for wedding bands, a wedding dress, and figuring out just how soon we could get our paperwork in for a license to be married in Oregon. On the boat ride back in, we decided we wanted to be married before he left on deployment—a seemingly stressful task for normal people, but he and I just wanted to be together.

Listening to Brian and me trying to sync our calendars together was almost comical as we looked toward the few weeks we had left together prior to deployment.

"OK, assuming everything goes according to the plan in place now, I should be flying out Friday, November 29. I'll be on travel this week and next weekend, so we could do it that week or the following weekend?"

"I have a work training that week so I can't then, how about that weekend? The 24th?"

We laughed at ourselves as we went about planning our wedding.

"We are probably the most laid-back bride and groom of all time. Who plans their wedding like this?" Brian asked, half serious.

"We do! Because we're awesome and we're doing it for us."

And with that, we had a date for our wedding. In the back of my mind was the fact that he would be gone for Christmas and I remembered a promise I made one night, while talking on the phone, when he asked me: "Ash, promise me we will never skip a holiday, OK? I want to always celebrate them with you." Keeping that promise—which I viewed as an act of love—was important to me, so we again looked at our calendar and saw that we had exactly three dates that weren't currently booked with travel, work commitments, and now a wedding prior to this deployment and started planning out the rest of our time together. We had a lot to fit into the next two weeks.

Saturday, November 16, Brian and I were pulling the fake Christmas tree we owned out of the closet under the stairs and taking turns sneaking upstairs to fill the stockings we'd decorated for each other earlier in the day. We spent the evening making chocolate thumbprint cookies, watching *National Lampoon's Christmas Vacation*, opening presents, and falling asleep in each other's arms in front of the fireplace. It was a memorable Christmas . . . albeit in November.

Brian had to go to Louisiana for work the week following our "Christmas" and we were quickly running out of time to pull this wedding off before his deployment.

November 12
5:51 p.m.
Hi Christina,
My name is Brian and I was wondering if you'd be available for a wedding Sunday, November 24th (sometime between 9am and 11am).
My fiancée and I live in Gig Harbor WA. I am active duty military and we want to have a small ceremony (really, an elopement) on the beach in front of the Sunset Surf Motel in Manzanita before I leave for deployment.
We will have about 5 guests there and do not require anything beyond a normal elopement type ceremony.
Would you be available for that day?
Thanks!
Brian
206-948-4459

He called me from New Orleans on Wednesday of that week to let me know he'd found an officiant who could meet us on Manzanita beach that weekend. It was extremely short notice, so we were excited and grateful she was going to make it work for us. Once we submitted the paperwork for our marriage license, we needed to make reservations at the Sunset Surf Motel in Manzanita and call the florist in Cannon Beach, who seemed caught off guard when I told her, "I need a small bouquet of flowers for my wedding . . . this weekend."

"I'm sorry?" I couldn't see her face, but by the tone she used, I could tell this wasn't a call she was used to getting. She had a million questions for me, what was my favorite flower, what colors did I like, what was the wedding theme, what color were my bridesmaids' dresses, etc.

"I don't have any bridesmaids, it's just my fiancé and me—and honestly I really don't care what they look like! I just want fresh flowers, maybe something with fall colors?" I gave her this one direction as she went silent on the other end of the phone. "I also need a matching boutonniere; can I pick them up Saturday afternoon?" I asked, hopeful she could make it work. "Well, this is certainly a first, but yes, I think I can do that for you."

We packed our bags and Chance, our rescue dog we'd adopted earlier in the year, and left our home in Gig Harbor on the morning of Saturday, November 23, and spent our four-hour car ride talking about our future, laughing at each other's ridiculous jokes, singing along to Cure songs, and anxiously awaiting being able to say *I do* the next morning.

Upon arriving in Manzanita, we checked into our motel before wandering down to the beach to meet up with Mike and George, our friends we'd invited down from Gig Harbor to celebrate with us. We sat on the beach in front of a bonfire, watching the sunset, exchanging embarrassing stories, and playing Never Have I Ever as we all passed around a bottle of cheap champagne. Eventually, long after the sun had set, we all retired to our rooms. Brian and I stayed up late talking about how unbelievably lucky we were and how we wouldn't change a single thing about this entire experience. We woke up the next morning, opened the curtains at the foot of our bed to views of the Pacific Ocean, and then had hot coffee and even hotter sex before starting to get dressed for our wedding. We stood on the balcony waiting for my two best friends to arrive, one of which would be taking our wedding photos, and we laughed in delight as they eventually appeared, driving down the street in front of our motel room balcony. Brian waved to them as the car drove by before suddenly realizing his mom was in the front seat of the car!

"Hey, there's Mike and Kasey!" he exclaimed, grinning at the site of Mike's silver family minivan headed down the road toward our motel. "That's so nice of them to come down here for this, they're such good frie—" He trailed off mid sentence and leaned forward against the railing, squinting his eyes to get a better look at the minivan. "Ash?" He turned to me, head cocked to one side, and looked back at the minivan to make sure he was seeing correctly. "Is that my mom!?" he asked, completely surprised but delighted to see her, knowing she'd now be here to be a part of his wedding day. We had previously decided not to invite any family members and only four of our very closest friends in order to keep it as low stress as possible, but it just didn't feel right not having our moms there, so I invited my mom and bought his mom a last-minute plane ticket from Boise to surprise him. It worked!

It was hands down the most relaxing, blissful, romantic, and perfect wedding day. We were married exactly fourteen days from the day he proposed to me, in the exact spot we had exchanged our first "I love you" nine months prior. We held hands, kissed, laughed, and cried together throughout our ten-minute ceremony on the beautiful, cold but sunny November day as we promised to always love, honor, and respect one another, to consistently put each other first and to always be partners in crime, until death do us part. We celebrated with lunch at the Sand Dune Pub alongside our few guests and then drove back to our home in Gig Harbor. Brian spent the next few days doing laundry and packing his sea bag while I protested his upcoming departure. We celebrated Thanksgiving that Thursday with a few of our friends and, by Friday, it was time to say our goodbyes as I took him to the airport to meet up with his submarine in Dubai.

Chapter Six

I'm not ready for this, I told myself while waiting in line with him to get him checked in at the airport. I knew that marrying Brian meant marrying into the military, but the gravity of what exactly that meant never hit until that day, that moment, at the Seattle-Tacoma airport. He was actually leaving. His orders didn't get canceled at the last minute as I had hoped. Uncle Sam didn't grant him a few more months with me just because we were a newly married couple. Nobody else volunteered to take his place on this deployment. I had been holding out hope that any or all of these scenarios would come true since the moment he'd told me he had orders for deployment. Standing there, holding his hand, tears stinging my eyes, I finally realized it: I was a military wife, this wasn't just my husband's career; this was a way of life for us both now and supporting him as my husband meant supporting his commitment to our country. However, as every military spouse can attest to, when you're about to watch the love of your life ship off, unsure of when you'll see or speak to him again, it's often hard to see it as more than a job and the fact that this job is taking them away from their family.

I started looking around me. There were so many people whose lives happened to cross my own path that day: people buzzing around the Delta airlines counter, juggling luggage carts, kids, and bags, lost in anxious conversation, glancing at their watches as if this would make the line go quicker. *I wonder if they know Brian is here to deploy. I wonder if that man over there, or that woman to the right holding on to her child, or that couple kissing by the sliding doors, are aware that Brian is here, waiting to get on an airplane that will take him away from me—his wife of a few days—just so he can protect our country for them. If only they knew . . . It's just not fair.*

"Ash?" Brian asked, keenly aware of how tightly I was holding on to his arm.

I averted my eyes so he wouldn't see the tears now uncontrollably streaming down my face as I grasped his arm even tighter.

"It's going to be alright, babe," he reassured me. "You're the strongest person I've ever met; if anyone can do this, it's you. And me. We're going to get through this. I promise you, OK?" And I believed him. I knew everything was going to be alright but that didn't make it any easier saying goodbye.

"Ma'am?" the ticketing agent asked quietly, not wanting to interrupt the moment Brian and I were having, but apparently from the use of Brian's military ID and iconic green sea bag he'd just checked in, she'd put together the goodbye that was about to transpire. "Would you like a gate pass so that you can walk him to the airplane?"

"Really?" Brian and I responded in unison as we looked up at her, tears now in both of our eyes.

"Thank you, sir, for your service," the agent said, looking directly at Brian before looking over at me and adding, "And for yours, too, ma'am . . ." as she bowed her head and wrote out my name on a small white piece of paper, which had just granted me an additional hour with my husband. What Brian and I were about to go through was not lost on people. It was something deserving of a thank-you and I was grateful. I smiled through my tears and accepted the generous token from her. This Delta employee gave Brian and me the gift of time and I will forever feel indebted for this small but impactful gesture.

We held hands tightly as we walked toward the security gate, a small sense of relief coming over us as we knew we were going to have a few extra minutes together before having to tear away from each other. I presented my gate pass along with my brand-new military ID—the very first time I'd had the opportunity to use it—to the TSA agent who looked it over and handed it back to me with a wink and nod in respect before he did the same for Brian along with a "Thank you for your service, sir." We walked through the central terminal of Seatac airport, toward the giant glass bay windows where we spotted two rocking chairs. We pushed them as close together as we possibly could, claiming them as our own, and we sat, holding hands, and trying not to cry—anymore.

"I'm going to miss you babe," he said. "We can do this though, OK? I promise I will write every day."

"Me too," I whispered. "Probably more than once." I smiled and looked up at him.

"It will be just like the smaller deployments we've been through, where I'll have access to sailor mail on the boat, but it might be a little while before you hear from me. I promise I'll be writing though, OK?"

"What do you mean?" I was caught off guard. "How come?"

"Because we have to be at periscope depth for the emails to be sent or received off the boat." He saw the worried look in my eyes, coupled with the fact I had no idea what periscope depth meant. "Basically, we have to be close enough to the surface to use the periscope and send or receive signals. This could happen every couple of days, but usually on these longer deployments it's more like a couple of weeks . . . sometimes a month." *A month!? I gasped but attempted to keep myself composed.* "We appear on radar anytime we use a signal like that and sometimes we go places where we don't want people to know where we're at." He looked at me and I think he could sense my sadness by the way I lowered my eyes and sighed. "Babe . . . don't worry. I will be writing to you, and I hope you'll write to me. That's what will keep me going out there, knowing you're OK here." He lifted my chin up with his fingers so he could look into my eyes. I smiled and kissed him. "Let's come up with a plan for our emails," he said proudly. "Since we might go a few weeks without receiving them from each other, how about we number them—you know like number one, number two, number three, number two hundred, and so on? Just so that, when the submarine pops up and we receive like twenty emails from each other at once, we'll know which order to read them in. Sounds good?"

"That's a good idea, babe," I said, feeling sad at the thought of not getting any communication from him for an entire month, but content with the fact we had a plan in place.

"I promise you I will be writing. Please try not to worry about me," he said, sounding as if he was trying to convince himself as much as he was me. "No matter how far away, no matter how long I stay, I will always love you. Right?"

"Right," I smiled, catching the song reference and letting it sink in. My mind began to wander again . . . *How many more times would we sit in these rocking chairs together, grasping hands and final moments before he shipped off on another deployment? He still had ten years left in the Navy before retirement and—*

"Just think that when I retire . . ." Brian said, interrupting my train of thought. *Did I say that out loud or was I just thinking that?* "We will have all the time in the world to go on as many adventures as we want. We can sail our boat down to the Galapagos Islands and go scuba diving!" My eyes lit up at the thought of us scuba diving in exotic places around the world. We'd been talking about wanting to get certified and—unbeknownst to one another—had actually purchased lessons for each other as birthday presents earlier in the year, but because of scheduling conflicts hadn't been able to take them yet. "We can travel wherever we want, whenever we want, and the Navy will take care of us for life; we just have to get through these hard years and then it's you and me, babe." We were rocking slowly back and forth, and I couldn't help but stare at him, as he held my hand and lost his glance in a horizon that existed only in his imagination.

We both smiled, knowing very well that nothing was going to stop us from turning that dream into reality.

"Promise?" I asked, seeing the same vision as he did for our future. "Only if we can get a couple of wooden rocking chairs like these when we're old and gray."

"You got it, babe, deal," he promised. "After we've sailed around the world and are ready to retire at the Oregon Coast, I'll buy you *all* the rocking chairs and we can sit together, hold hands, and watch the sunset."

We stood up and started walking toward the gate when we heard, "*Good morning, ladies and gentlemen, this is the boarding announcement for Delta flight . . .*"

Oh no . . . the knot in my stomach suddenly became very noticeable. Was this really it? It can't be . . . I'm not ready. It didn't matter though; the time had come to let him go. We embraced one another and stared for a long time into each other's eyes as the tears made their way back.

"*We would like to first welcome aboard passengers that need a bit more time, including those traveling with small children, as well as our active duty military passengers . . .*"

We walked slower than two people have probably ever walked toward a jetway in an airport before, but we didn't want to let go of each other's hands and we weren't ready to say goodbye. We moved to the side and stood there, both of us with tears streaming down our cheeks.

"I love you. I hope you know that, Ash. I love you so much. I'm always coming back home to you. You know that, right?"

"I know, babe. I love you too. I'm so proud of you, but I'm going to miss you so much," I said, trying to appear strong, but wanting him to know how much I was going to miss him. Thoughts of brides shipping their husbands off to wars for decades prior flashed through my head as we stood there. Time had certainly changed the circumstances over the years, but the emotions we were both feeling were there, and it was terribly hard to pull away from one another.

"I love you."

"I love you."

We gave our final embraces before I had to let go and watch him walk down the jetway. He turned to wave goodbye and send me a kiss before disappearing into the airplane.

I cried the entire walk back through the airport, toward my car, and the thirty-minute drive home. I was a mess. Every time I stopped at a red light, I read the text messages Brian was sending me, telling me how much he loved me and how much he was going to miss me. "They're about to close the doors, babe, I have to turn off my phone. I promise I'll be safe and I'll write every chance I get. Remember, I'm always coming back home to you." I put my phone down and continued my drive home, ten miles down I-5 and across the Tacoma Narrows Bridge, toward Gig Harbor, wiping tears and mucus on my sleeve before pulling into the driveway of our light blue house, where our sweet dog, Chance, was waiting anxiously to greet me.

It was rather early still, but I had to get ready to go to work and I certainly couldn't show up with bloodshot and puffy eyes from all the crying. After taking a quick shower, I sat on the floor of my bedroom, throwing a ball for Chance. "This sucks, bud. You're the man of the house for the next few months, OK?" He looked at me—tilting his head from side to side—offering his support in a way only a dog knows how to. Even though the morning had been a very intense and emotional one, I felt somewhat relieved that the hard part of saying goodbye was over and we were now able to start the countdown until he came back home to me. *Ugh, even this coffee tastes gross without him here*, I thought as I placed the almost-full cup into the sink. I must have really drained my energy from all that crying. I looked through the cupboards for a quick breakfast, but nothing looked appetizing; in fact, I realized I was even a little light-headed as I took a second glance, but I was running late, and I had to get to work. "Be a good boy today, Chance. I love you! I'll be back in a little bit," I said as he walked me to the door and I gave him a final head scratch, locking the door behind me. *Alright, Ash, pull yourself together*.

As soon as I arrived to work at the bank, two of my coworkers, who also happened to be military spouses—and had lived through their own deployment goodbyes before—greeted me at the double doors and wrapped their arms around me, asking how I was holding up. It took all I had not to start crying again, but I felt a sense of comfort wash over me in their presence. They knew what I was feeling, they'd been in my shoes before, and more than likely would go through it again in the future. I was one of them now, a military spouse with a deployed husband.

"Oh, honey, I'm so sorry. I know how hard this is," Linda began.

"Will he get post-deployment stand-down when he gets back? Maybe you could plan a trip for the spring when he's home!" Tara knew how much Brian and I loved to travel and had been through countless deployments with her own husband who was in the Army, so she was doing her best to cheer me up.

"You can come hang out with me anytime! And Robert can help you with anything you might need help with around the house while Brian is gone," Linda added, volunteering her husband—unbeknownst to him as he was at work with the Air Force. "Honestly, what's helped me the most when Robert's been deployed is to get into a routine. Every military spouse does it differently, but I promise you this will make that countdown go a little quicker. And it will help Brian to know that you're doing OK at home so that he can focus on what he needs to do out there. You can do this, honey, he knows you can, otherwise he wouldn't have chosen you. Brian is serving the country while out to sea, but you're serving it by supporting him. Remember that, OK? And when you can't, I'll remind you." Linda was a seasoned military spouse, and a person I trusted. She was a fountain of wisdom and I knew I could rely on her for anything that had to do with the military—and friendship—during this deployment period.

"Just landed in Dubai! I miss you! I love you!" The text message appeared on my phone as I sat next to Chance on the couch later that night after a long day at work. I grabbed it, a giant smile already across my face, and hurriedly wrote him back, *"Hiiiiii! I miss you! I love you!!!"* Brian would have a few days in Dubai to acclimate and get final orders cleared up before loading onto his floating home for the next six months: the USS *San Juan*. We spent these few days talking on the phone and keeping in touch via text messages because we knew that, once he shipped out, it would be months before we'd hear each other's voices again. I knew he'd have a few days in town but due to the secrecy of submarine movement, he wasn't able or allowed to tell me when he'd actually be shipping out. All he could tell me was, "We can talk for a few more days, and then I'll have to say goodbye, OK?" When Sunday came and went and he was still texting me, I was thankful, but he'd left three days ago, and I knew those few days of getting to talk to him from afar were quickly coming to an end. By Sunday night, my stomach was still in knots, I felt exhausted, and I was even a little nauseous as Chance and I settled into bed. *Either my body is having a physical reaction to being this sad, or I'm coming down the with flu. I hope Brian didn't get it before he left . . .*

I texted Brian before I went to bed Sunday night that I wasn't feeling well and worried I might be coming down with the flu. I woke up Monday morning for work and had to sit down in the shower because my head was spinning. *Oh great, this really is the flu.* I didn't have a fever and I wasn't throwing up, just slightly nauseous and a little spinny. I knew we were short handed at work that Monday, so I thought I'd go in and get everyone set up—and head home early if I needed to. Linda and Tara could tell I wasn't feeling well and tried their best to help me get through the day as quickly as possible while keeping their distance in case I was contagious. I was happy when I realized I'd made it to closing time and couldn't wait to go home, put my pajamas on, and cuddle up in bed with Chance.

After about an hour spent in bed, I began thinking through my flu symptoms. I realized I hadn't eaten much that day—nothing had sounded good. For the past few days, the opposite had been true: every time I opened the fridge, I had to close it in fear of getting nauseous at the sight of the food inside. Even the smell of my morning coffee had turned my stomach. "Ugh, of course I would get the flu now, Chance," I said while scratching his head. But I didn't have a fever. And I hadn't actually thrown up yet. And I hadn't been around anyone recently that had the flu; where could I have caught it from? And then . . .

No way.

"Chance! Dude. What if I'm pregnant?" I said as I suddenly sat up in bed, making Chance jump up from his sleep. *Nah, that's not possible.* "It's not possible, right?" I asked Chance, who tilted his head while looking at me.

It was possible. My thoughts immediately flashed back to the conversation Brian and I had had while in San Francisco for my grandma's funeral.

***

"You're going to be such a good mom," Brian whispered in my ear as we sat together—a few drinks in—at the Fiddler's Green Irish Pub near Fisherman's Wharf. My brother Zack and cousin Peter were on the barstools next to us, the man in the corner was playing an Oasis cover song on his guitar, and we had just toasted to the memory of Grandma Isabel.

"What!?" I gasped, not expecting those words to come out of his mouth in that moment.

"I mean it. Seeing you around your family these past few days and witnessing how much you all love one another, and how you try to take care of everyone. I want to have a family with you someday," he said, looking me in the eyes and grasping my hand as if to emphasize how serious he was.

"The next round is on Brian!" Zack shouted from his barstool next to us—interrupting our current conversation—with a full pint already in front of him.

"To be continued . . ." Brian whispered to me as we joined the celebration Zack and Peter had already started.

After a competitive game of cribbage on our flight home the next day, Brian, having just won the game, must have been feeling pretty confident because he looked up at me and said, "I was serious about what I said last night. I want to have a family with you."

"I know you were, babe. And just for the record, I think you're going to be a great dad too. All the preschool moms are gonna be so jealous," I teased him. We began talking through the what-if's and the how's, what we wanted for our future, as individuals, as a couple, and now potentially as a family. "I've been on birth control for so long though, it will probably take us a while to get pregnant."

It was decided in that ninety-minute flight home that we were ready to start a family with each other.

***

"Want to go with me, Chance?" I asked while I pulled on a sweatshirt. He quickly jumped off the bed, stretched, and waited for me by the door. *It's got to be the flu. Right? There's no way I was pregnant. I'd only been off birth control for one month and Brian had JUST left on a six-month deployment. There's just no way.* Chance and I drove the few miles down the road to the nearest store where I parked the car and walked in.

"Welcome to Walgreens, can I help you find anything?" the cashier greeted me.

My cheeks flushed red and I bowed my head, slightly embarrassed at my reason for a visit. "No, thank you!" I exclaimed louder and faster than necessary as I did my best to avoid eye contact and made my way toward the pregnancy test aisle. There were suddenly so many in front of me. *Why are there so many different brands? What's the difference between the pink box and the blue box? What is HGC? Why do I care about the levels of it?* I was overwhelmed but getting more and more excited about the prospect of what that ten-dollar test was about to tell me. I couldn't decide on one, so I grabbed four of them before checking out—trying to avoid the judgy eyes of that same cashier—and ran for the car.

"This is crazy," I told Chance, back home and laughing at myself, as he awkwardly watched me try to pee on the first pregnancy stick, certainly getting some on myself in the ridiculous process. *Who invented these tests anyways? This is a terrible design flaw!*

"OK, Chance, three minutes," I said as he watched me put the cap on the stick and place it on the counter. The instructions had been very clear that the results were not accurate until the full three minutes had surpassed, so I pretended to not look as I watched the white screen slowly display one faint pink line . . . and then the faintest hint of a second.

"Wait . . ." I said in complete shock, a smile as faint as the double line in front of me forming on my face. "Is that a line?" I grabbed the stick and brought it closer to my eyes to make sure my sight wasn't betraying me. "Chance, is that two lines!? But two lines means I'm pregnant . . . why would there be two lines—" I began shaking. Chance and I stayed in my bathroom as I took a second test. And a third. And the fourth. Each had varying shades of pink and blue lines; one even had a very faint + sign on it. *There's just no way.* I ran downstairs as fast as I could and googled: "Why would a pregnancy test show positive if you aren't pregnant?" Google basically answered back: "It won't."

"Chance. I think I'm pregnant," I said out loud, more to myself than to him. *Oh my god. I'm pregnant. I'm pregnant? I'm pregnant!* My husband was eight thousand miles away, about to be trapped under the ocean in a submarine for six months with very limited communication, and I had just found out we were expecting our first child. I raced to my phone and I was about to call him when I remember it was the middle of the night in Dubai.

"FACETIME ME AS SOON AS YOU WAKE UP!" I texted him. Hoping the capital letters would be enough to show him how urgently I needed to talk to him. I went back upstairs to check on the pregnancy tests and make sure that second line hadn't faded while I'd been downstairs. They were all still there; according to these tests, I was *still* pregnant. One hour later, my phone came to life as I saw *BJ My Hubs* flash across my phone screen, meaning he was awake and had received my urgent text.

"Ahh, it's Brian!" I nearly yelled at Chance, who had fallen asleep on the couch next to me. I answered his FaceTime call with the screen turned toward the pile of positive pregnancy tests.

"Are you OK, babe? What's up?" he asked, puzzled—still groggy from sleep and still in bed with the lights off. I kept the camera pointed toward the tests to give him a moment to register what he was looking at. I couldn't see his face since it was completely dark in his hotel room, but I began to hear the laugh he did when he was nervous or excited about something. "Babe, what's that?" I could hear a mix of excitement and anticipation in his voice as he realized what he was looking at.

I turned the camera around and, beaming from ear to ear, I told him: "I'M PREGNANT!"

He turned the light on. I was greeted by the site of his chestnut brown hair flowing in every direction, thin red creases on his face from where his pillow had been pressed against him, and the slightest hint of crusted drool on the corner of his lips. Years spent on a loud submarine had taught him to sleep well and sleep hard. He sat up in bed and I watched those words sink in. He put his hand over his mouth, an expression of shock on his face, and a big, bright smile quickly formed on his beautiful lips as he laughed sweetly into the camera. He couldn't believe it. I couldn't believe it.

"No way . . ." he said, beaming from ear to ear. "Is that for real?" The excitement was building in his voice as he began processing the same feelings I'd been for the hour leading up this call.

"I took four of them and they all say yes. Babe, I can't believe it!" I responded, as tears began to well in my eyes. Our lives were changing during the course of this conversation. Our first baby was on the way.

Chapter Seven

Deployment sucks. There's no other word that effectively sums up my feelings on the subject, other than, it sucks. The TV shows and movies that portray military spouses looking out the window with a single tear dripping from their eyes while longing for their husband, American flags and bald eagles proudly flying in the background while patriotic music plays—what a crock. We did have an American flag flying on our front porch, but the similarities began and ended there. The tears streaming down my face were plentiful and often accompanied by pieces of peanut butter toast being regurgitated during terrible bouts of "morning" sickness, which lasted all day—and night. The baby growing inside of me had me dizzy, nauseous, and emotionally unbalanced while the military had my husband deployed with varying degrees of accessibility to send emails or communicate with me. I constantly had my phone at my side, waiting for it to chirp indicating I had a new email.

My only saving grace during these long, hormonal days was Mike, a military member in his thirties who had been renting a bedroom in our home since January and had quickly become one of our dearest friends, as well as one of the distinguished guests at our very small wedding. He had also been left with strict instructions from Brian before shipping out: "Please take good care of Ash." Mike quickly became the Will to my Grace. We found ourselves to be hilarious, while Brian, and Mike's boyfriend, George, did their best to tolerate our shenanigans. We bonded over our dogs, Chance and Lily; our loves, Brian and George; our delightful sense of humor; and more often than not, our mutual love of junk food.

"Mac and cheese for dinner?" he'd ask when I'd walk in the door from work.

"Can we do fancy mac and cheese?" I'd shout back as I made my way upstairs to change out of my work clothes.

"You got it," he'd say, laughing, understanding the term we'd come up for when making boxed macaroni and cheese, but adding grated cheddar cheese and black pepper, making it feel and taste . . . well, fancy.

"Is it my turn or yours to DJ tonight?" I'd ask after coming downstairs in my sweatpants and Brian's gray USS *Ohio* sweatshirt he'd left for me again before shipping off.

"Hmmm, I think it's your turn. But I do have a new song I want you to hear!" he'd say as he took control of the computer we had in the attached dining room. This would kick off our festivities for the evening where we'd go back and forth, sharing control of the computer mouse while singing along to songs we'd play on YouTube.

I spent all other free time writing emails to Brian, filling him in on the projects Mike and I had done around the house, talking him through the pregnancy milestones we were reaching—our baby growing from the size of a poppy seed to a raspberry, then a lemon—and trying to stay connected, no matter how far apart we were physically. Brian went through this pregnancy with me, every single step of the way, albeit while in a steel tube, miles under the ocean surface. He affectionately referred to our growing baby as "our little poppy seed" up until the day we were finally reunited, and he saw that she was indeed much bigger than a poppy seed. We had been married less than one week before he left on deployment and we were now navigating life as newlyweds—as well as our first full deployment and first pregnancy together. Emails became our lifeline while he was gone and how we stayed emotionally connected to each other during one of the most exciting and trying times of our life.

December 7, 2013
6:35 p.m.
#2 & #3
USS San Juan

Hi babe!!! I love you and miss you so much. I looked at our wedding photos today and it literally hurt my heart because I miss you so much. I hate being away from you. It's gonna be even harder when our baby is born. Luckily, soon, I can be on shore duty and I'll be home every night.

I'm glad that Chance and our lil poppy seed are keeping you company. Your Mom wrote me the sweetest note—seri-

ously, so cute! She said she's coming up and she's going to play Santa and you gals are gonna do some festive stuff. I'm sure with a grand baby on the way she's super stoked and will be up at our place a lot. Maybe it's a good idea to have a big guest/grandma room, haha! I'm sure we'll need it.

Things are going well here. I'm being safe, don't worry about that. Actually, playing a lot of cribbage and reading. So, super exciting on my part. Haha. I do miss you terribly. I haven't opened any of my cards yet, I'm holding out for a bit longer until I start doing that. I haven't run yet, probably going to do that tomorrow morning. It's kind of hard to find a good time to do it when no one is up. Probably early morning is a good bet.

How are you feeling lately? Have you noticed any changes in your body? I'm sure it's probably a bit too early to tell.

I can't even express to you how stoked I am to be married to you. And then, add on top of that, WE ARE HAVING A BABY!!! Haha . . . seriously. So stoked!!!

Ok, gonna sign off now. I love you madly. Always and forever.

Brian

December 24, 2014
1:17 p.m.
#37
USS San Juan

Hello my wife!

Today, December 24th, is our 1 month anniversary! Happy Anniversary!

I wish I could be there to give you a month's worth of married kisses, but I'll just have to make up for them when I finally do get home.

I love you more than anything in the world.

Have a good anniversary day and know that I'm looking forward to a lifetime's worth of happy months with you.

All my love, always and forever,
B

December 31, 2013
9:22 p.m .
#48
Gig Harbor, WA

My love!

It's New Year's Eve and Chance and I are at home on the couch. :) people around us are lighting off fireworks but Chance isn't even barking! He's such a good pup. He's cuddling at my feet as I write this to you. We miss you!!!

Today was a rough day for me . . . I spent the better part of the day being really nauseous and having to sit in the back room at work. I'm feeling better now that I'm home and relaxing, but it sucked earlier. I'm confident I'll start to feel better soon though :) my belly is getting so big!! Wait until you see it! I can't wait to have you run your hands in my belly and to feel our little poppy seed in there!

Mike sent me a text today saying he's back in town but up at George's! It'll be nice to have him home again, the house is so quiet when it's just me and Chance! Plus I have some projects I need his help with. :) I prolly won't tell him that until he gets here though, just to make sure he still comes home. :)

We're gonna head to sleep in a minute but wanted to say hi and let you know how much we miss and love you. I looked through all the pictures on my camera today and it made me miss you so much. Your cute little face and your smile that I love so much. I hope you get home to me soon, it's torture being away from you!!

I love you!!

Ash <3

January 1, 2014
6:26 p.m.
#49
USS San Juan

Hii MOMMY!!!!!!!

I love you! I'm so excited to see our lil kiddo! I'm so so so happy that everything looks healthy too. I was getting a little concerned that maybe that wouldn't be the case, but I'm so excited and so relieved that you and the baby are healthy!

I was thinking they would do a sonogram, but I wasn't sure. I read that in some of the books I bought. I'll have to read up about the next appointment though, I hadn't worked that far yet. How are they supposed to test the baby?! Do they stick you with a needle?!?! And how in the world do they know from that if the baby is gonna be ok? And I think you're even more right to say that it's going to be healthy and beautiful and happy!

Getting these emails from you about the appointment makes it even more real . . . I can't wait to see the photos and videos. And, even more, I can't wait to be a parent with you!! We're gonna be awesome parents. Speaking of which, I was reading one of the sailing magazines you sent me—one of the articles was written by a schoolteacher turned world cruiser about home schooling your kids while sailing around the world. I want to check out her website when I can . . . I forget what it is now, I'll send it to you later.

I'm not sure when I'll be near shore again. When I am, I'll be super excited to hear your voice though! I sure love you. And I'm BEYOND excited the video of our poppy seed's heartbeat!! Just to think of it brings a huge smile to my face.

Today is New Year's Day. So, big whoop. I've never liked New Years anyway . . . not much of an exciting time for me. Not sure why. I'm glad you just hung out at home and didn't do anything. You deserve as much down time as you can get to stay rested and well.

Ok babe, I'll write more later. I can't wait to be around internet and be able to call and talk to you!! You and this baby are THE MOST important things in my life —always. Please don't forget that. And don't forget that I'm thinking about you all the time and that you and I love you!!

All my love, always and forever;

B

February 24, 2014
7:00 p.m.
#111
USS San Juan

Hey babe!

Today is the 24th of February. I've been writing you once a day because there's not a whole ton going on and I could write about 48399 times a day but it would be to tell you that I love and miss you. Mostly cause that's how I feel: all the time.

I hope you're feeling pretty good, today is almost 16 weeks! Can you believe it!? Time has really gone by hasn't it. I'm sure you're probably thinking I'm crazy for saying that and that it's been dragging on, huh. It won't be long and we'll get to find out if it's a boy or a girl. I'm still holding out for a girl. Did you know that submariners usually have girls? Something about being around more radiation or something like that, but guys that have been on submarines for a little bit usually have girls. I'm not sure that it's based on science or any sort of fact, but I know A TON of guys from work that have girls, mostly after they've been on a boat for a bit. So, that's my two cents. Get ready for a girl! :-)

How do you feel about me starting a blog about being a new dad when I get back? Is that something you'd be ok with or would even want to contribute to? It might be fun to document what we go through and the decisions we make to help other people out. Kind of like a virtual social group. I know I read people's blogs when I have questions about stuff like this. What do you think? It's something we could do together, like "New Mom and Dad Blog", etc.

I know we're gonna be awesome parents and I can't wait to be home with you. You make me so happy. I love you babe. I hope things are going well for you. Have you been eating and sleeping ok? I think about you all the time. I've been gone almost 3 months now. :-/

All my love,
B

March 19, 2014
7:34 a.m.
#116, #117
USS San Juan

First of all, I LOVE YOU. I can't express that enough.

So, names for our BABBBYYYYY!!! I'm stoked, I can't wait to have this little munchkin running around tearing up the house!

Boy: Hudson
Girl: Isabel

These are the middle names I like in order of preference

Boy:

#1. Atticus
#2. Asher or Nicodemus

#3. Blakely
#4. James, Hawthorne or Newport

Girl:

#1. Claire or Charlotte
#2. Blakely

I REALLY like Charlotte for a middle name for a girl. Or Claire. Those are my top two for a girl middle name. For a boy middle name, I like Atticus the most. Or Asher. Asher means happiness, it is from the Bible. So, there's that. Not sure how you'd feel about that. So is Nicodemus and I'll probably use that for a pen name when I start pumping out best-selling novels to support us as we sail around the world.

It's about noon here and I think I'm gonna go work out soon. I sure do miss you sweetheart. You make me so happy. I LOVE YOUUUU!!!!!

B

Brian's deployment was going well—for him. He worked long, irregular hours on the submarine, and would spend his downtime working out in the makeshift "gym" onboard—exercise equipment stored between torpedoes and in cramped hallways—and writing me emails telling me about his days at sea, things he was thinking of, dreaming of, and looking forward to doing upon return.

"Babe," he wrote me once, "everyone that I talk to at work says that their lives stopped when they had kids and they didn't go do anything or have fun for a few years because the kids came and made leaving the house difficult. They also keep making jokes about how we won't be able to afford the boat anymore . . . telling me I'll have to sell it. They obviously don't know me . . . or you very well."

I shook my head and rolled my eyes, knowing how sailors at sea like to give each other grief, and particularly teasing Brian about what was to come with his new life as a father. However, the joke was on them, because while we would end up selling *Time and Tide* shortly after Brian's return, it was only in preparation of buying a newer, bigger boat that would accommodate our new life as parents—and have plenty of room for a baby, and any additional ones we might add down the road.

When I finally reached the five-month pregnancy mark, it was time to schedule an anatomy scan, during which we'd make sure everything was on track and in the right spot with our baby, and also hopefully find out if Brian's premonition that we'd be having a girl was accurate. My midwife knew Brian was deployed and gave me a window of time of when I could schedule the appointment—in hopes Brian would be pulled into port somewhere in the world during that time frame and we could find out together, via FaceTime, if we'd be having an Isabel or a Hudson.

"Mike. What should I do?" I asked that night over some fancy mac and cheese.

"Hmm . . . and you can't push it back any further?" Mike had been deployed on numerous occasions with the Air Force and was keenly aware of how unreliable port calls and deployment schedules were. "What if you schedule two separate appointments so that if he's not in port for the first one, you can cancel it and still keep the second one? I know he can't tell you when the boat will be pulling in, but maybe try emailing him and see if he can give you an idea of when you should schedule it for," Mike suggested.

"It's worth a shot, I'll try that. If he's not in port and we can't find out together, you're going to have to be responsible for keeping the secret. You know that, right?" I teased him—but not really. That night, I emailed Brian my scheduling window and asked if he thought he'd be in port at all during that time frame, and then I waited. And waited. And waited. Two weeks passed without a single email from him, so I went ahead and scheduled my anatomy scan for Wednesday, March 12, 2014. In a strange alignment of stars—and Navy schedules—after over sixty continuous days underwater with very little contact, I received a phone call from our ombudsman (the Navy liaison who keeps spouses of deployed sailors up to date on port calls, important matters, etc.), saying the USS *San Juan* would be pulling into port *somewhere* within the week and I should expect a call from Brian shortly. I immediately called my midwife to push back the date of our ultrasound, now knowing I could stretch back the date just a little bit, so he'd most likely be in port and able to find out the gender of our baby together!

A strange number appeared on my phone a few days later and I picked up the phone to hear, "Babe, I'm in Bahrain! I miss you!"

Brian was safe and on dry land. It had been months since I'd heard his voice and my heart was bursting. We spent the next few minutes exchanging "I love you" and talking about my growing belly, how I was feeling, and what the latest news was.

"I rescheduled my ultrasound appointment hoping you'd be in port for it. Babe, I'm so happy! Now we get to find out what we're having together! You're eleven hours ahead of us right now though, so it's going to be at two a.m. your time. I know you are going to be exhausted, is that alright?"

I knew from his emails that he'd been sleeping very little, and when he *was* sleeping, it was on a thin mattress, on top of an uncomfortable metal shelf, in the torpedo room of a submarine. I was asking a lot by having him give up one very precious night's sleep in his hotel room in Bahrain while the boat resupplied, but we were about to find out if our little poppy seed was going to be an Isabel or a Hudson. "I wouldn't miss it for the world, sweetheart. I'll set my alarm for two a.m., just FaceTime me when they're ready," he told me from half a world away.

Two days later, my full bladder and I arrived at the doctor's office and waited for my name to be called.

"Ashley Bugge?" a woman in pink scrubs called.

I got up as quickly as I could, considering I was carrying around a bowling-ball-sized belly, and walked behind the technician, cell phone clutched in hand.

"How are you doing today?" she asked casually.

I sat down on the paper-coated exam table, looking directly at the "No cell phones" sign taped to the wall and started in on the speech I'd been rehearsing in the waiting room.

"Well, I'm OK, but my husband is currently deployed . . ." I began, hoping she would take sympathy on Brian and me and the circumstances preventing us from being at this appointment together. "Oh, honey, I'm so sorry for you"—I continued with how I found out I was pregnant right after he had shipped out—"Oh, sweetheart, that must have been amazing and awful at the same time"—how I hadn't been able to talk to him for weeks, sometimes over a month at a time—"Oh dear, you must miss him so much"—and how he knew I was at this appointment today but . . . "it's the middle of the night where he is right now, but he's set his alarm and I know you're not supposed to have cell phones in here, but we really want to find out what we're having together . . . is there any chance I can FaceTime him right before you tell me?"

I was confident I had tugged at all the right strings and hopeful she'd grant me my wish. "He's missed all the pregnancy milestones so far, so it would mean so much . . ." I added as I adjusted myself on the bed, lifting my shirt up, exposing my round belly.

"You aren't supposed to use cell phones in here," she began quietly, "but I won't tell if you don't tell." She followed with a wink.

Bingo. My impassioned speech had worked, and I was over the moon.

"Let's start with some measurements and I'll tell you when it's time to give him a call, OK? And please thank him for his service. I'm from a military family, too, and I know you have to take these moments when you can get them." I was near tears as she placed the warm ultrasound goop on my belly and images of our little poppy seed appeared on the screen.

After listening to the baby's strong heartbeat and taking all the measurements, I was surprised when the technician said, "Alright, if you'd like to call him, the baby is in the right position to reveal the gender."

"Really!?" I was ecstatic. This was the moment we'd been waiting five months for.

She nodded and smiled at me. I could see it in her eyes she knew what we were having. I couldn't wait anymore. I grabbed my phone and began calling Brian on FaceTime. My heart was racing and with each ring that went unanswered, my breathing became heavier. *Come on, babe, wake up. Answer your phone.* It was all I could think about.

No answer.

I looked at the technician and apologetically explained it was almost two a.m. where he was. I was going to try again.

Ring. Ring. Ring. No answer.

I tried a text message. *Babe! Are you awake? I'm at my appointment and the ultrasound lady is ready to tell us what we're having! Can you please call me???*

No response.

I knew Brian was a *very* heavy sleeper, but I was determined to wake him up no matter how many times I had to call him—I tried again. And again. And again. No answer.

The ultrasound tech took sympathy on me and offered to finish her exam, saying she knew what we were having and I could try calling one more time at the very end to see if he'd answer. I agreed and she continued on with her exam while I continued to send text messages halfway around the world.

I was anxious. And frustrated. And sad. And—

"Hello?"

"BABE!" I yelled at the sound of his groggy voice. "You're awake!" My tone a mix of excitement and frustration.

"Oh my gosh, sweetheart, I'm so sorry," he said, still a bit on the groggy side. "What time is it? Did I miss it?"

"No," I said, laughing. "But you almost did. I'm here now and we're just finishing my appointment."

Brian turned the light on in his room—his eyes still full of sleep and the corner of his mouth showing a little drool.

"Alright, so, Dad, did you want to listen to the heartbeat first?" the tech asked.

"Really!? Yes . . ." Brian managed to say, overwhelmed with emotions.

Lub-dub-lub-dub-lub-dub-lub-dub . . .

Brian brought a hand over his mouth as his eyes filled with happy, happy tears. As I saw his reaction, I became emotional as well.

"Oh my god . . . that's our poppy seed . . ." he whispered.

"Alright," the technician began, "if you guys are ready . . ."

I inadvertently held my breath.

"It's a . . ." I watched Brian through the lens of my camera, eyes wide with anticipation and his lips slightly parted. "It's a GIRL!"

And in that moment, across the world from one another, Brian and I laughed and then cried together via FaceTime, relishing in the fact that this baby growing inside my abdomen would soon be our daughter. We'd recently settled on the name Isabel Blakely, her first name after my grandmother and her middle name after our favorite sailing destination in the South Puget Sound. My husband was eight thousand miles away, but I'd never felt closer to him.

***

March 19, 2014
2:09 p.m.
USS *San Juan*
Hey babe!! How are my girls doing?!

Guess what . . . we're having a baby girl!!!

I'm so excited, I've thought about it about 4883983 times today!

Isabel Blakely—so darn cute! I'm already starting to worry about her. Haha, like dad type stuff worry. We'll need to buy a shotgun within the next 10 years—I'm already planning for that one. It'll be a mean lookin' shotgun too.

I've told a bunch of people at work and they are all excited for us and think the name is great too! I'm so lucky to have you sweetheart, you're amazing. Thank you for being so strong and loving, I know this is not an easy thing for us to do—me being out here. Just remember, this too shall pass.

I think your ideas of blue, yellow, and white for her room is a great idea. Maybe we should both start compiling a list of the things we'll need to get done before she gets here and then when I get home I can start working on some of those things. Off the top of my head, I've got:

#1. Get rid of my extra "treasures" (i.e., crap).
#2. Paint her room.
#3. Baby-proof the house.
#4. Make love to my wife a bunch.

Those should keep us busy for at least a bit, especially number four.

But, seriously, I don't want to spend the time I have off working just messing around, I know there are a ton of things that will need to get done so we can be prepared for her arrival. Those are things I can do while you're at work on my days off (except #4). Don't worry, I plan on

> *doing some stuff to relax, too, going for bike rides/runs, etc. Maybe swimming at the Y.*
>
> *Anyway, just thinking. Ok babe, I love you. I'm so glad we got to find out together that we're having a lil' girl! I love you!!!*

***

The weeks following were consumed with helping Tara and Linda plan my baby shower, finishing up projects around the house with Mike, and preparing our dog, Chance, for the fact that he wouldn't be an only child anymore. We had most everything in place, except for the date of when Brian would be coming home to me.

Our emails continued as the deployment went on. "It sounds like they don't have our flight details all ironed out yet," he wrote one day, "but from what I hear it'll be a late flight, but who knows, things change all the time. I know you're excited for me to come home, heaven knows I'm so stoked too. I can't wait to hug you and kiss you and feel Izzy bouncing around in your belly! I'm sorry that it's been such a pain with not being able to tell you when I'm coming home for sure. I wish I were coming home tonight, but it'll be in no time—it'll go by fast! And plus, you have Izzy's first baby shower to look forward to! I can't wait to see what kinds of sweet things we get!"

That evening, as I tried to get comfortable in bed, Chance next to me, I smiled while rubbing my growing belly. It was hard to believe I hadn't seen my husband in almost six months, that when we'd last held hands and hugged, saying goodbye at the airport, I was his skinny(ish) new bride, and now I fell asleep, six months into our marriage, a giant belly containing our first daughter. I didn't have an exact date, but I knew there were only a few more days left before we would finally be reunited. Only a few more days until Brian would see this belly, feel his daughter kick his hand, and experience life as an expecting father in person. Only a few more days until I heard his laugh and held his hands. Only a few more days . . .

Chapter Eight

"Hello?" I said anxiously into the receiver, recognizing the Navy ombudsman's number flash on my phone screen.

"Ashley? It's Kari. Can you chat for a minute?" she asked, as if there was any chance in the world I wouldn't have dropped literally anything I was doing to take that call, knowing full well what it meant.

"Is he coming home!?" I smiled into the phone.

"He's coming home." She smiled back. "The boat should be in port within the next few days and he can give you a call as soon as he's in. I don't have his flight information yet, but I'll let you know as soon as I have it."

Oh my god, he's coming home. I've waited six months to hear those words and now I had them. I let it sink in. He's coming home.

Two days later I was just putting my phone on silent and settling into my desk at work when my screen flashed *unknown number* indicating an incoming call. Call it a military wife's intuition, but against the side glance from my boss standing next to me, I answered that call with a feeling it might be him.

Please don't be a sales call. I really don't need to review my car insurance right now. "Hello?" I said, a hint of optimism in my voice.

"Hi sweetheart, how are you?" his sweet voice crooned.

"Babe! I knew it would be you! You're coming home!" I smiled through tears as I made eye contact with my boss to let him know I had to take the call before seeking privacy in the back room of my bank branch.

"I'm coming home." I clung to his words as I closed my eyes and pictured him on the submarine dock, standing proudly in his navy blue uniform, sun beating down on him, hand running through his thick brown hair, black boots scuffed up from months at sea, and giant grin on his face knowing he was finally coming home to his family.

"I didn't get any flight information from your command, do you know when you'll be home?" I asked anxiously. "Our baby shower is Sunday! Do you think you'll make it home by then?"

Tara and Linda had been working diligently on planning a shower for baby Isabel and me, and with family and friends traveling in from out of town for the event in just a few days, moving dates wasn't really an option, so I was hopeful Brian would somehow make it home for the event.

"Let me check in and see if they've confirmed tickets yet, but I'll try really hard. Who all is going to be there? Is your mom coming? My mom? Uncle Mike?" Brian had already missed so much of this pregnancy, he didn't want to miss a single more second if he could help it.

"I love you," I whispered, as I opened my eyes to the small silver clock on the wall. In this moment, 9:07 a.m. on a Friday morning in the break room of the bank I worked at, I realized Brian and I had experienced the highest highs and the lowest lows together through these random phone calls from around the world. From the death of my grandma, to finding out we were having a baby girl together, from port calls during the beginning of our long-distance relationship, to hearing his voice telling me he was coming home after this excruciatingly long deployment, some of the best and the worst moments of our relationship had come from phone calls from random numbers, at various times of the day, and this phone call, in this moment, was no different.

My thoughts were interrupted as I heard chatter in the background of his phone and he begrudgingly said, "I have to go, babe, I will call you as soon as I'm in my hotel and cleaned up, OK? I love you!"

"I love you, too, please call as soon as you can! And let me know as soon as you have your flight info!" I added, hoping the reminder would somehow make him get home faster.

I spent the next ten minutes in the safety of the back room crying happy tears and daydreaming of my husband. It had been a long six months, but hearing him tell me he was coming home erased every hard day I'd had since our initial goodbye. A sharp jab to my ribs from Isabel jolted me back to reality, reminding me I was at work as I wiped my eyes and opened the door, stepping out toward my desk.

"Ash! Was that Brian?" Linda yelled across the bank lobby. I looked up and couldn't wipe the smile from my face long enough to respond. She didn't need me to say it; she had received calls from her deployed husband to the same effect and knew what that smile meant.

"Oh, sweetheart! Is he coming home? When?" She sounded as excited as I had felt hearing his voice moments prior.

"He's coming home," I cooed. "I don't know when yet, but he's coming home."

Brian called later that evening to tell me his flights were worked out and while he wouldn't be home in time for our baby shower on Sunday, he'd be home a few hours afterwards, in time to kiss me and my swollen belly good night.

The next few days dragged on . . . and on . . . and on. The countdown had begun, and Sunday couldn't come quick enough. Tara and Linda showed up to our home in Gig Harbor, arms loaded with hors d'oeuvres, pink balloons, silly games, and diaper cakes, fully prepared to host the best baby shower possible. Brian and I had built this incredible community of family and friends, and I couldn't help but laugh as I watched this particular group in our living room, blindfolded and feeding each other applesauce from baby spoons in the name of our unborn daughter. I laughed and took photos of the ridiculous game, wanting to savor the moment for what it was, but also glancing at the clock and hoping time would speed up. Soon enough the baby shower was over and I was grabbing the Subaru keys and driving over the Tacoma Narrows Bridge on my way to the airport where Brian would see my pregnant belly, and his daughter—in utero—for the very first time.

Wearing a white knit sweater, which accentuated my baby belly, I approached the same security gate Brian and I had entered six months prior during our goodbye, this time with a bouquet of American flag-themed *Welcome Home* balloons in my hand as I stood with a smile on my face, anxiously shifting my weight from one foot to the other as I waited for a faint sight of him. "Just landed!" appeared on my phone screen and I quietly told my belly this was it, she was about to meet her dad for the first time. "I'm outside of security, hurry!" I wrote back as I inched my way closer to the double doors, currently the only thing separating me from the love of my life, as he made his way to me, to us. I moved the bundle of balloons to my other hand as I stood on my tippy-toes, raising my chin, moving my head slightly left and right in search of Brian, who should be appearing any moment. I took a deep breath, trying to calm my heart rate, when at last, the sight I'd been waiting for: dark brown hair, blue eyes, dimple on left cheek, and giant smile on his face. Brian! *He's here.* The most handsome man I've ever seen, and he was walking toward me, his wife. I couldn't wait a moment longer, I took off running—OK, waddling—ignoring the security barrier and guard standing on the other side. Brian stopped in his tracks at the sight of me running toward him and held his arms outstretched as I leapt into them. We were both suddenly in tears, our bodies and lips embraced as tightly as possible, savoring this sweet reunion. We had waited six long months for this moment and here it was, in the middle of the airport security exit.

"Not cool!" the TSA agent yelled from her post. "Keep moving!" she urged as we locked our arms around each other and tried to make our way toward the exit, not willing to separate our grip from one another.

We moved to the side while those around us watched our reunion with keen interest as I pressed my head on his chest and he lowered his chin to kiss my forehead. Oh, his smell. His warmth. His embrace. At that moment, I had no idea how I had survived so long without him.

"I told you, didn't I?" he whispered.

"Told me what?" I looked into his eyes, which were filled with happy tears.

"I'm always coming back home to you."

Life had continued on while Brian was gone, and I'd figured out how to manage it by myself, but now that he was home we needed to find our new schedule and really how to do life with each other again, in person. The adjustment period is a chunk of time well known in the military community by service members and their spouses, following a long deployment during which everyone works to find their new routine, together. Mundane things you don't often think of had to be relearned; boxed mac and cheese with Uncle Mike—even if it was fancy mac—wasn't going to cut it for dinner anymore. Things like sharing the TV remote, dirty towels on the bathroom floor, asking about weekend plans, sharing the covers on our bed at night, even falling asleep with a body in bed next to each other was something we hadn't experienced in six months and took some getting used to again.

Soon, however, our lives were back to normal. Brian had quickly become very hands-on with the pregnancy, drawing me warm baths on Friday nights, informing me of which milestones Izzy was reaching in her growth, and getting on my case whenever I didn't follow doctor's orders to take it easy. The last bit of my pregnancy I'd been suffering from gestational hypertension and my doctor was concerned it would lead to preeclampsia, so at thirty-five weeks pregnant she prescribed bed rest for the remainder of my pregnancy. Having a doctor's note to miss work, enjoy the fact that it was Girl Scout cookie season, and watch as much trashy reality TV as I wanted seemed like a wonderful way to enjoy the last few weeks of my pregnancy, except, there's only so much keeping up with that K family I could do, and I was restless. Brian had always adored and admired my independent spirit, until it came time for him to support, *errrr,* enforce me staying on bed rest. He'd leave for work in the morning but knew me well enough to give me a call on his drive in to make sure I was in fact taking it easy.

"Ash, I'm almost to work. What are you doing? Are you in bed?"

"Yessss . . ." I would reply coyly, pans clanging together in the background as I stood in the kitchen making breakfast.

"I know you too well, get back in bed!! You heard what the doctor said," he'd counter in his concerned tone.

"Ugh, babe, but I'm so bored!" I complained, but I knew he was right. "Alright, alright . . . Can you call in sick the rest of the day and come hang out with me instead?" I'd ask, half teasing, mostly not.

"I wish, babe. You just sit your cute little butt on the couch and I'll take care of you when I get home." I could hear him smile in response, knowing how stubborn I was, and that he'd have to call another three or four times that day to remind me to get back in bed.

Aside from the threat of pre-eclampsia—something my doctor kept a close eye on with regular checkups—the third trimester was moving along well, and in fact we were approaching my due date.

At thirty-seven weeks pregnant, I suddenly began experiencing a lot of swelling in my feet and spikes in my blood pressure, so I went in for a fetal non-stress test and to check on baby Isabel. "Ashley," my midwife began, "your blood pressure isn't coming down and with the other symptoms you've been experiencing, I think it's best if we go ahead and induce you."

"OK." I looked up at her, nervousness now spreading through my body. "When?"

"My nurse just called the hospital and we can get you checked in at 4:30 p.m. today."

"Today?!" I sat up straight in the chair as her words began to register. "As in, we're having this baby *today*?!"

"Yes. You'll have time to go home and get what you need, call Brian, make sure you eat something, and then go to Labor and Delivery and we'll get you settled in," she clarified.

I hopped off the table, wiping the ultrasound gel off my stretched-out belly, and walked toward the exit, frantically searching my purse for my phone to call Brian and share the news.

I dialed the number to his desk as fast as I possibly could and counted each ring tone until I heard his voice: "Det UUV, Chief Bugge, how can I help you?"

"Babe! It's me! I'm just leaving my appointment, can you talk?" I asked, trying to hide the sound of panic and excitement from the news I'd just received.

"Hey! Yeah, what's up? Everything OK?" I could hear the sudden concern in his voice.

"Any chance you can come home now? It turns out we need to go to the hospital . . . you're about to be a baby daddy!" I said, laughing through tears.

"What!? Today!? Seriously?" He was shocked but I could hear the smile forming on his lips as he registered this news.

"Yes, today!" I was trying my hardest not to shout in excitement as I walked out of the lobby, into the July heat and toward my car. "We're supposed to be there to check in at 4:30 p.m. *Agh, babe!* I can't believe it, we're about to be parents!"

Brian raced home from work and together we threw a random assortment of personal and baby items into a go-bag before texting Uncle Mike to let him know we wouldn't be home that night and asking if he'd look after Chance for the next few days. We hopped in the Subaru and made it nearly halfway to the hospital before realizing neither of us had eaten lunch yet and we weren't confident the labor and delivery department of the hospital would have anything vegetarian for us to eat. We talked ourselves into a quick stop at Red Robin restaurant and were just ordering our Boca burgers when my phone rang with a number I didn't recognize.

"Hello?"

"Hello, is this is Ashley Bugge?"

"Yes, this is she."

"Mrs. Bugge, this is Sarah calling from Tacoma General Hospital. We had you scheduled to begin your induction at 4 p.m. today, were you still planning on coming in?"

"What!?" I choked on the sip of water I'd just taken. "I thought we were supposed to be there at 4:30! I'm so sorry, we're just having lunch but can be there in thirty minutes, is that still alright?"

"No problem, I will move the schedule around a little bit and we'll see you at 4:30," she responded, thankfully sounding somewhat amused.

I hung up quickly and met Brian's questioning gaze. "That was the hospital, she said we were supposed to be there at four! We're running late for our own baby being born. Who does that?!" We exploded in laughter together and made comments about this being one of those moments for the memory book.

Excited and nervous now, we quickly got in the car and made our way to the hospital, our cheeks a shade of light red as we said our names and reason for visit at the reception desk. Brian inquired if one of the coveted LNDR (labor, delivery, and recovery) rooms we'd heard about on our hospital tour was available—he was particularly interested in this room because it had a large bathtub and flat-screen TV—but much to his disappointment the specialty room was not available at check in, which meant he'd have to forgo his planned bubble bath while I labored. Once settled in, I was hooked up to monitors, IVs, and a handful of color-coded wires, and shortly after that, Brian and I were watching in new-parent awe as the contraction monitor began moving back and forth, indicating baby Isabel was on her way here.

We spent the next eighteen hours playing cribbage, talking about our dreams for baby Izzy, and napping when we each could. It had been a long day, and an even longer time since lunch, and I was starving. Against Brian's better judgment, I ordered minestrone soup and sipped the broth, which took approximately twenty minutes to come right back up, as my body contracted and my sweet husband held a green plastic puke bag in place as best he could for me. Soon after this less-than-glamorous moment of my life, with minestrone-streaked hair, I turned to Brian to tell him I could feel her coming and it was time to push. It took less than four minutes of hard pushing when all of a sudden, she was here. Isabel Blakely Bugge, born July 21st, 2014, and weighing seven pounds, eleven ounces, was now a part of our family in a moment that had forever changed our lives. Brian cut her umbilical cord before she was wrapped in a blanket and placed in his arms as he beamed from ear to ear and said, "She's here, babe!"

Eat. Play. Diaper. Sleep. Repeat.
Eat. Play. Diaper. Sleep.
Eat. Play. Diaper.

Sleep? Sleeping quickly became a thing of the past as our entire household immediately became protective over this tiny human Brian and I had created. We all took turns holding baby Isabel, talking to her and pointing out the little furrow she got between her eyebrows indicating she was about to laugh, cry, or poop.

"Your turn to change her, Uncle Mike," Brian would tease, pretending to hand Izzy over to her adopted uncle for a diaper change.

"I don't remember signing that line in my rental agreement," Uncle Mike would tease back.

Twenty-one days later in a yellow sun bonnet and matching onesie, *Daddy's First Mate* printed across the front in blue block letters bought specifically for the occasion, we set out on *Time and Tide* for our first afternoon sail as a family of three. Brian and I had been looking forward to this moment for the past nine months. We had created a life for ourselves revolving around the ocean and it was important for us that Izzy and any future children feel this same connection to the sea as we did. We spent the afternoon out on the Sound, the warm July breeze gliding our boat effortlessly through the water as we took turns holding Izzy and the helm.

Brian turned to me, a look I can only describe now as pure happiness on his face, and said to me, "Want to know how to tell when you've officially made it?"

"How?" I asked, smiling at him.

"This moment right here."

Chapter Nine

"Happy birthday, babe! I might be more excited about giving you this present than you are, but you're going to LOVE it!" I was near tears, on the edge of my seat as I handed Brian the envelope containing his birthday gift. I looked over at Uncle Mike, who was joining us for Brian's birthday festivities and was the only other person who knew what was inside the envelope.

"Just rip it!" I couldn't wait a second longer; the anticipation had been building and I wanted to see the smile on his face when he registered what was inside.

For as long as Brian and I had been dating, he'd had a flyer on his refrigerator in bright red and white letters, *Learn to Scuba Dive! Dive Oahu $99!* His uncle had bought him a book on scuba diving when he was ten years old, and he'd been obsessed with the idea of diving ever since, exploring the unexplored, being a part of the sea, but he'd never taken the time to do so. Until now. In the spirit of *No Bucket Lists* and knowing this was something he'd wanted to try since he was ten years old, and something I knew I'd love to do as well, I'd bought the two of us diving lessons for his birthday. I sat anxiously as I watched him peel the sticky backing of the envelope, peeking through trying to figure out what might be inside. I looked at Uncle Mike, who winked at me, privy to my excitement, and back at Brian as he pulled the certificate out.

"We're going diving!" I yelled, extending my arms, expecting him to jump from his chair into them in a gracious show of affection.

Brian looked up. From me to Uncle Mike and then back to me. "Noooooooo," he said, taking much too long to say that word than was necessary. He looked at Uncle Mike sitting next to him and asked, "Well, now what should I do?"

O-kay, this certainly isn't the reaction I was expecting.

"Huh?" I said in a state of shock. "You don't like it?" I asked, my excitement quickly fading to disappointment.

"Aw, no, I love it, babe! I really do! It's just that, um, you should open your birthday present now too," he said as he stood up, walking to the fridge, and grabbing a large white envelope from the cupboard above.

"What are you talking about? My birthday's next month. Babe, I thought you'd be excited about your present. I've been waiting weeks to give this to you!" I said, the disappointment evident in my voice.

"I do love it! I'm so sorry, sweetheart, I didn't mean to react that way. I do love it, so much. Seriously, you know I've wanted to go diving since I was ten, this is the most thoughtful gift you could have given me. I'm serious, I want you to know that, I love it."

Not sure what to say and taken off guard by Brian's sudden idea to exchange birthday gifts on *his* birthday, I simply stood there and watched him walk back toward me with an envelope similar to the one I had just gifted him. We both looked up to see Uncle Mike giggling to himself, obviously keen on what I was about to find inside.

"Happy birthday, babe!" he said as I looked up, catching a quick sight of the dimple on his left cheek.

I slowly opened the envelope, still unsure of why I was opening my own birthday present in this moment. He brought his hands together by his mouth, his eyes wide open with anticipation. The slower I opened the envelope, the harder his top teeth bit into his bottom lip. Finally, the envelope was open. I peeked inside and saw what looked like a gift certificate.

"Are you *serious*?!" I couldn't believe it. "Is this for real?" I erupted in laughter. Holding in my hands, I had the *same* certificate for scuba diving lessons I had gifted to Brian for his birthday.

"You guys are ridiculous," Uncle Mike interjected from his chair, laughing at the fact we had bought each other identical birthday presents. "You guys each told me that's what you'd bought one another, and I came so close to telling you, but was hoping I'd get to witness this moment so I kept my mouth shut. Who surprises each other with scuba diving lessons?"

"We do!" Brian and I responded in unison, erupting in laughter again.

We booked and canceled our scuba diving lessons a half dozen times over the next few months due to Brian's work schedule. He was now working on the USS *Houston*, a submarine whose current home port is in Hawaii, which meant in order to get his project and team ready for their next deployment, he was traveling back and forth between our home in Gig Harbor and Hawaii at least twice a month. While the long-distance demands of this schedule may be a hindrance to some families, we saw it as an opportunity to do some traveling and have adventures together as a family, in Hawaii!

For the next six months of our lives, Isabel and I flew back and forth between Washington and Hawaii at least once a month, long enough to visit with Brian, have a mai tai (or three) at the Barefoot Bar in Waikiki, and enjoy this new exotic lifestyle we were living as a transpacific family, willing to fly six hours across the ocean to spend time together. We fell in love with Hawaii and all that it had to offer us as a family. We'd spend our mornings walking the beach, daydreaming about moving there someday, how we could sail on our boat to the other islands, meet up after work to go surfing, and even though we'd previously had to push back our scuba diving lessons in Washington, this seemed like an ideal place to learn.

On our third trip over in just as many months, Josh, a sailor that Brian had previously deployed with, and his wife, Brenda, who were now stationed at Pearl Harbor, offered to watch Isabel for us one afternoon so that we could finally do our Discover Scuba Diving class. We drove down to Kewalo Basin Marina, met our divemaster for the day, filled out our waiver, got fitted with our wetsuit, buoyancy compensation devices, attached our weight belts, fins, and masks, and we were soon on our way out of the marina and into the open ocean. We had been briefed at the marina and on the boat ride over about some basic hand signals and skills we'd have to practice once in the water before moving on with the dive, and we felt pretty confident we'd know what to signal if any of us saw a shark. Before we knew it, the boat had grabbed its mooring ball, our air tanks were turned on, we were tapping the tops of our heads indicating we were OK, and just like that, our first splash as our fins hit the water. We spent the next hour exploring an area off the coast of Waikiki known as "The Pipe" looking for sea turtles, octopuses, and humuhumunukunukuapua'a (the Hawaiian state fish). Soon it was time to surface, peel out of our suits, and head back to the marina. That dive, that single hour of our lives, forever changed us. Brian felt it, I felt it, and we knew this wouldn't be our last time in the water scuba diving together.

"Where should we get certified?" Brian asked as we finished out our epic date day with a heaping plate of hot and spicy edamame at the Waikiki yard house.

"Hmm . . . we could do it here on your next work trip? Or we could go somewhere cool and try to fit in a vacation while we're at it," I offered, biting into the spicy soybean pod, savoring my favorite dish on the island.

"I should have stand-down between Christmas and New Year's at work, we could try to go then. That doesn't leave a lot of time, but we could probably get down to Mexico and back? I think the course is four days long and then we could dive for a few days afterwards." Brian was a changed man after experiencing the ocean in the way we just had and he was ready to get certified, now.

"Sure! I'll see if my mom can watch Izzy and we could fly down the day after Christmas and home after New Year's." I pulled up the calendar on my phone, making sure we didn't have any scheduling conflicts between our jobs or family obligations. "It looks clear, let's do it!"

Two months later, Brian and I were in Playa del Carmen, shaking hands with Juan, our Mexican divemaster for the week, the man who would introduce us to the incredible sport of scuba diving, who would share his expertise and passion of all things ocean with Brian and me, and the man who would quickly become a dear friend and diving mentor of ours.

We spent the week driving from our rented studio apartment in Playa del Carmen to destinations all around Cancun, Tulum, and Cozumel. We'd wake up early, often making love in the sweltering apartment, before putting on our bathing suits and walking down the stairs to the communal kitchen.

"Cheers, babe!" Brian said as he held out his cup of coffee.

"Cheers!" I said, smiling as I tipped my cup over to his, leaning in for a kiss. "I can't believe we're in Mexico learning to dive, this is the coolest. Thank you for being my adventure partner." We both grinned, grabbing a piece of fruit and a couple of peanut butter and jelly sandwiches to last us through the day before reaching for our sunnies and heading out the door to meet up with Juan.

We spent the first few days in class learning the basics of how to "breathe" underwater and how to signal danger to your dive buddy. We learned terms like decompression sickness, the importance of maintaining proper buoyancy, and the importance of respecting your gear, your fellow divers, and the ocean.

Brian and I had never experienced a thrill as exhilarating as the one we felt when we went scuba diving. We knew from day one that we were hooked. We never wanted to get out of the ocean; with each kick of our fins, we felt like we had found a part of ourselves while in the water. Brian was fascinated by the technicality of it all; he loved learning how things worked, the proper way to maneuver his gear, how taking deep and shallow breaths could help control his buoyancy. I'd often look over and find him hovering above the coral, forty pounds of air tanks, weights, and gear on him, but weightless in the water. I was drawn to the sport for the challenge and allure of it all. This unknown and undiscovered world that only a portion of the world's population will ever get to see. Absolutely nothing in this world compares to seeing sharks and manta rays—

creatures we'd previously only seen at aquariums or watching *Blue Planet* on TV—in their natural environment. During these training dives, Brian and I would take turns tapping on our air tanks to get each other's attention, pointing out the brightly colored sea anemones, giant grouper, and every once in a while, one of us would spot an elusive octopus. We were certified as open water scuba divers on December 31, 2014, in an underwhelming ceremony put on by Juan where he gave us each a handshake, pieces of paper with our names on them, and a reminder to always keep our "bubbles up." We spent the next day, New Year's Day 2015, doing our first official dive as certified divers with Juan and his wife, diving the Dos Ojos cenote—a system of caves and caverns spanning thousands of miles underneath the Yucatan Peninsula—in Tulum, Mexico. We spent the evening eating fried avocado tacos while watching the sun set over the ancient Mayan ruins, thankful for the experiences we'd had, but ready to head home to our daughter and the opportunity to dive in our own backyard of the Puget Sound.

Chapter Ten

Once home from Mexico, it didn't take long for the military to remind us we were part of something much bigger than ourselves as Brian came home from work one day to say his next deployment had been scheduled and he'd be shipping out in a few weeks. The sense of pride I felt for my husband's dedication to his career and his desire to serve our country never wavered, but these conversations were always hard. The knowledge that he'd have to deploy again is a different feeling than having an actual date we'd have to say goodbye, and as always, he wasn't able to tell me much about where he'd be going or for how long he'd be gone. Taking him to the airport was just as excruciatingly emotional as it been previously, but this time I didn't have the luxury of breaking down because our little girl needed me. So, I told myself I had to be strong for the both of us.

We knew it would be another six(-ish)-month deployment, which meant he'd most likely be gone for Izzy's first birthday. We exchanged tearful goodbyes with a promise to write as soon and as often as possible. Emails had become such an integral part of our relationship, a way of life for us over the years, yet my heart still raced every time I heard my phone chime, his name appearing in my inbox indicating a new email.

***

From: Brian
To: Ashley
Date: Sun, May 3, 2015 at 12:57 a.m.
Subject: #4
Heyyy sweetheart!

It makes me happy to hear that you think I'm special; I hope you know that I know that about you too, babe. We have an amazing relationship. Something I wouldn't trade for the world. You are the best wife and mother that I could ever ask for. It makes me so happy to hear you talk about your daughter and how much love you have for her and how proud of her you are. That just makes me love you even more.

That is hilarious about Izzy and standing up in the crib! I should have lowered it before I left . . . I can't believe she's already to the point where she's standing up in there! Before we know it you're going to write to me and tell me that she's walking!!!! Wow! She's growing up so fast it's nuts. But it makes me a little happy too because soon we're going to be able to teach her to do awesome stuff and she'll become her own person. Actually, she already really is her own person. Such a huge personality. I can't wait to watch her grow up and be a part of her life.

That's so sweet that you've been telling her stories about me. That puts a HUGE smile on my face, I hope you know that. You should totally take her to the zoo or aquarium, I think that's a great idea. She should grow up appreciating animals and loving them like we do.

I love you so much sweetheart. I'm thinking about you all the time. Give our cute kid a kiss for me and know that my love for you grows more and more each day.

Always yours,

Beej

From: Brian
To: Ashley
Date: Thu, May 7, 2015 at 11:21 a.m.
Subject: #8

Heyyyy sweetheart!!

I love you too!! I look forward to getting your emails so much.

I hope you have some fun while I'm gone. I agree; we have so much fun together. Our life is awesome! We seriously have the best life.

Every time you talk the hammock I get so jealous! I wish I could be there with you to get to hang out in it. Sounds so awesome. How's the garden going?

No, right now it's not stressful at all. It will be in a few weeks though.

That's so funny about Izzy. I miss her so much. She's such an awesome kid. I was looking at a photo of her the other day with me and her in it and I said the same thing; she's got my hair, my ears, my nose . . . but she has your eyes and TOTALLY a huge part of your personality. She's so smart. So sharp.

I have a great idea that I'm going to do when we pull in. One of the guys I've been working with out here on the boat did this. He got a bunch of kid's books and recorded himself reading them and then sent them home. So, I'll do that too. And I can mail the books home so you can show her the book while I'm reading it. And I can just email the movies back home and you can play them on your mac. Great idea huh?!

I can't wait to hear your voice babe. I really miss you. I'm sure you're doing well . . . it sounds like it.

> Ok babe, know that I love you and I'm thinking of you!
>
> Always yours.
>
> Beej

***

Brian had been deployed a few months when a travel deal popped up in my email: *14-day Australia & Fiji, airfare included $2,499.* To be fair, I received these travel alerts daily but tried not to click on them because it made me want to buy them—I'm pretty sure that's the genius behind this marketing technique—however, it was hard to book vacations this far in advance without knowing my husband's travel and deployment schedule. Yet, this time I took the bait and opened it up. Brian and I had recently been talking about how incredible it would be to dive on each of the continents, and Australia in particular had a certain allure to it with its white beaches, great visibility for diving, a romantic destination for Brian and me to make adventurous memories together.

I closed the browser and walked away from my computer. I checked to make sure Izzy was still sleeping, walked downstairs to get a glass of water, looking for things to distract myself with, before finally walking back upstairs, knowing full well I was about to book that trip.

"Hi, is Matt there?" I asked, my voice shaky, suddenly nervous to be making this phone call to Brian's work.

I heard the shuffling of work boots, paperwork being moved across a desk, and then the sound of the handset picked up. "Berginc," the voice on the other end of the line said.

"Hey Matt, it's Ashley Bugge, Brian's wife." I coughed, even more nervous now. Trying to remember why I thought making this call to Brian's boss would be a good idea.

"Oh hey, Ashley, is everything OK?" he asked, his tone softening as he realized I wasn't a coworker or superior calling asking him to do something.

"Hey, yeah, everything is great. I'm so sorry to call you and I'm not really sure of the rules with all of this, but I want to surprise Brian with a trip to Australia in December and I know his travel schedule is all over the place, but he's obviously deployed right now so I can't ask him about it and the deal I found expires in three days . . ." I was rambling. I could hear myself and knew I needed to get to the point. "I'm calling to ask if you think there's any chance he'll be around and able to go on the trip? I know it's subject to change, and I'll buy travel insurance just in case, but I was just hoping you could give me either a definitive no or a maybe, otherwise I'll buy it and just cancel if we need to." *Whew. I'd done it.*

"Oh, wow. Yeah, I don't think we currently have anything on the calendar for December and I know he'll just be getting back from deployment so we can always try to trade some stuff around to try to get him out there. I guess if you buy travel insurance and know plans might change, I don't see why not," Matt responded, much more calmly than the frenzied tone I'd asked with.

We talked on the phone for a few more minutes as he checked in on how things were going with Isabel and me and letting us know he and the rest of the detachment were there if we ever needed anything. I hung up the phone, a giant smile on my face, and hit "Book Now." *We were going to Australia and Fiji!*

***

From Ashley
To: Brian
Date: Fri, Jun 12, 2015 at 12:05 p.m.
Subject: READ ME & RESPOND IF YOU CAN!

I found a KILLLLLLER deal to go to Australia December 1st-15th. It includes flights and hotels and a 4-day trip to Fiji in there too! Should I buy it? There's only 3 days left on the deal. I know I can buy travelers insurance and I called Matt at your work to make sure you could take that much time off in December, he said he didn't see a problem with it. GAHHHH I hope I hear from you!!!!!

PS. I love you!!!!!

From Ashley
To: Brian
Date: Thu, Jun 18, 2015 at 3:56 p.m.
Subject: #49

IZZY TOOK HER FIRST STEPS TODAY!!!!!!!!!!!!!! They were just tiny little baby steps, and I had to bribe her with veggie chips to do it, but she took them and it was SOOO cute!!!! I took a video of it and sent it to your cell phone so you can see when you pull into port! Can you believe it!?! I mean I know she's been close to walking for a little bit now but she finally did it! :)

I got 2 emails from you today! They were dated over the past 2 days so I hope that means you're getting all of mine too. In one of them it said you received one dated May 25th - today is June 18th so it looks like there's a little bit of a lag. :)

I miss you babe. I wish you could tell me when I'm going to get to talk to you. It would be so nice to hear your voice and see your face. <3

I still haven't gotten an email from you saying you know we're going . . . until then I'm a little nervous that you don't know!

OK baby I'll write more later tonight, just wanted to tell you about Izzy!!!

WE LOVE YOU! <3
xoxo

***

It was a solid two weeks after I'd already booked our trip to Australia and Fiji before I heard back from Brian: "I'm totally stoked for Australia too. Seriously. I can't wait. Talk about the trip of a lifetime. It'll be so amazing. I want to see and do as much as we can, as long we get in some good diving days. I know there is a TON to do there though." Between working full-time, raising our daughter, writing Brian emails, a hefty travel schedule, and testing my entrepreneurial skills by starting a new business as a wedding officiant—something I had a lot of fun doing at my brother's wedding— days turned into weeks and weeks turned into months.

Before I knew it, Brian had been gone for three months already and we had a solid deployment routine down.

From: Brian
To: Ashley
Date: Sun, Jun 14, 2015 at 7:28 a.m.
Subject: RE: #23

Heya sweetheart!
It's almost June 5th. You probably won't get this awhile though. The last email I got from you was dated the 25th of May . . . I think I could mail a letter to South Africa faster, haha! But it's better than nothing. I love you so much and I'm thinking of you and Izzy all the time. I was laying in my rack the other night thinking about Isabel and how she's going to be ONE YEAR OLD soon! I can't believe that much time has already gone by, but at the same time a ton has happened, you know? It's been a busy year.

It makes me really happy to hear that you enjoy hanging out with my sister so much. That's awesome. I REALLY REALLY like that we enjoy spending time with each other's siblings. That's so huge! And to watch the cousins play and laugh. I can't wait to look at all the photos of them playing and having a great time.

Nice job on getting Isabel new clothes! I'm sure she will be looking snappy for the summer . . . I can't wait to be home to get to hang out with you two! Is the weather getting warmer yet? Are you having massive hammock & firepit hangout sessions?! I would be. I'll bet my mom LOVED getting to spend time with Isabel one on one. She sure loves that kid . . . but who wouldn't!? She's about the best thing ever. I'm a little worried that our next one will turn out to be a tyrant! Haha, we totally have the best kid ever. I'm sure that our next one will be a girl too . . . Just so you know.

How has the Australia planning been going? Oh, when are you going to Alaska? And when are you going to California? Did you decide on NY yet . . . when is that again July? Dude, Isabel needs to open up a frequent flyer program. For real. We need to be getting POINTS! Ha

I can't wait to come home! OK babe, I gotta run. Please know that I'm thinking of you all the time and I love you so so so much. I can't wait to be home with you and our adorable little girl! Give her a giant hug and a kiss for me. ALLLLLLLLLL my love, always and forever!
<3 B

From: Brian
To: Ashley
Date: Thu, Jul 30, 2015 at 12:49 p.m.
Subject: RE: 63 & 64

Heyyyy babe!
I get your emails and it's crazy . . . you seriously have SO MUCH going on! I know it keeps you busy but I do worry about you. I am so proud of how much you're kicking ass! I

wish I could be there to help too, I feel like you're seriously bootstrapping this business up from the ground and making it happen and that has to be so satisfying. Who knew there was so much opportunity for Wedding Officiants?

I know it's a ton of work, I watched my mom bootstrap multiple businesses as a kid. And now I'm watching you put all sorts of time into this thing. What I don't want is for you to get burned out or learn to hate it or anything like that. I do want you to take care of yourself! We don't have a time limit or anything like that; we don't rely on this business to provide for food so we can take it nice and easy. What locations are you thinking you'll want to open? Are you thinking in Washington/Oregon or somewhere else? Maybe California would be fun.

Things are going well here. I think I pretty much say that in every email. Nothing too crazy. Just kind of taking each day and making it through. Did some paperwork today and some brief making, etc. Very exciting. Mostly waiting to get started.

I said in my last email that we are getting close to not being able to send or receive emails so please don't be surprised. I'll keep writing though. I have one last meeting to go to then I'll be hitting the rack. I sure do miss you a ton.

Ok babe . . . I gotta run. I love you so much. Please give Izzy a hug and kiss for me. I hope you got my email about

going to the Oregon Coast when I get back for a family vacation. What did you think about that?
Always and forever . . . all my love!

B

***

One day while at the grocery store with Izzy, my phone rang. I rifled through my purse to see an international number on the screen, which could mean only one thing.
I scrambled to grab the phone, abandoning my shopping cart and stepping to the side to take the call. "Hello?"

"Babe!" Brian always sounded on top of the world when he was able to call me from foreign ports. "I have great news!"

"Hi! Oh my god, where are you?!" It had been a few weeks since I'd heard from him so I wasn't expecting him to be in port and certainly wasn't expecting a call from him right now.

"The submarine needs to have some repair work done, so it's pulled into port for the month!" he could barely contain his enthusiasm.

"Wait, what!? Where are you? Can Izzy and I come see you!?" After three months of not seeing my husband, I was elated knowing he was on dry land and my first reaction was to buy a plane ticket to wherever he was in the world to spend as much time together as possible before he'd ship out again.

"Even better," he said.

Huh? I thought. But I didn't have time to turn this thought into spoken words because Brian shouted over the phone: "I'm coming home!" I swear I could picture him throwing his hands in the air, a giant smile on his face. "It would be too expensive to keep us all here for the month, so we're coming home and then we'll fly back out for the last half of deployment. It means the schedule gets pushed out on the back end, but…"

"Are you serious?!" I cried out loud, interrupting him and completely forgetting about my shopping cart full of groceries.

"Yes!" he said. "And guess what that means—"

"You'll be home for Izzy's first birthday!" I didn't let him finish.

I would have flown absolutely anywhere in the world if it meant getting to spend ten minutes with him, but it turns out this time I wouldn't need to: my love was coming home.

Chapter Eleven

After celebrating Izzy's first birthday together, we reluctantly said goodbye to each other again as Brian had to go back to the submarine and finish his deployment. I kept myself busy by writing emails to Brian, getting ready for our trip down under, taking care of our now one-year-old daughter, working full-time, and managing issues as they came up at home, including engine issues with our sailboat, *Time and Tide*, which we discovered on an afternoon sail during Brian's short visit home.

From: Brian
To: Ashley
Date: Sun, Aug 23, 2015 at 8:14 a.m.
Subject: 8/20/15

Hi babe.
The last email I got from you was dated on 8/3 and I received it on 8/13. I know you feel the same way so it's kind of like preaching to the choir; but it's REALLY hard being away from you and not getting to talk. Some guys here never write their families. They say they don't have anything to say. That's hard for me to fathom. I love our date nights where we go down to Tides and watch the boats drive around and eat pizza and drink good drinks . . . and just talk. Those are my favorite. I miss you so much. I can't wait to get to spend time with you and Izzy soon. It's crazy how alone you can feel out here with so many people standing around you. I don't really get to talk to anyone out here like you and I talk, which is to be expected. I'm sure I'm not the only one. But, it still makes it hard to not get lonely.

I feel like I'm always complaining . . . I just miss you. That's what I really mean to say. I miss you

I opened one of your cards today; the one with the anchor stamp on it. It was talking about the boat and how many awesome memories we have on it and how we will make more. It's true though . . . I can't wait to get home and make more memories on the boat with you and Izzy. It's going to get increasingly harder to keep her out of trouble on the boat though. Especially as she learns to walk! We will have to make sure to get her a good life jacket. I know it would be super hard to sell the boat we have now; but I wouldn't be too heartbroken to get a nicer/bigger one that would be comfortable for us as a family to get out on for longer periods of time. The only reason I bring that up is because of the engine. I know I talked about this in other emails so it probably seems like I'm repeating myself, especially as you read all of these emails roughly in the same time period. Hopefully that guy looked at the engine and he said he'd be able to fix it for a decent price that doesn't involve having to replace the engine. If we have to replace the engine, we'll need to talk long and hard. Look at some numbers and make a solid game plan on what we want to do.

In any case, I'm looking forward to sailing with you and Izzy again soon! The photos you put in there made me happy . . . looking at how tiny Izzy was and us carrying her around while sailing and still making amazing adventures together as a family. That stuff makes me very happy. I did work out today. Just not feeling well, over all. It was an ok workout . . . I think I'm going to start running over lunch breaks, when I get back to the office. I think that'll be a good time to do it so that when I come home we can spend time together. But, I do want to get back into running a lot . . . Train for a half marathon again.

Ok babe, I should get going. I love you so much and miss you like crazy. All my love.
Beej

From: Brian
To: Ashley

Date: Tue, Sep 8, 2015 at 1:18 p.m.
Subject: RE: 103

I can't believe that first phone call was almost three years ago. So crazy. Time has flown by so quickly. This is almost the end of our second deployment. And our two-year anniversary in just a couple months! Wow. And we have a daughter who is over a year old. Actually . . . she's 13.898393938 months old. I just counted. :-)

My love. You make me so happy, even from so far away. Just knowing that you're waiting for me at home, with our beautiful daughter, makes it all worth it. I know that someday we'll look back on these days apart and know they were difficult but worth it. Times that taught us just how strong our love is. I know it's a bit trite to say it but; nothing good comes easy. And I know that this love we share is beyond good. It's beyond words that can express anything good . . . they're just not enough.

I think we have more than a shot at it . . . I think we have it. As long as we keep being who we are as individuals then we'll keep growing as a couple and that will only prove to make us stronger and more in love each day.

I promise I'm hurrying as fast as I can. I can't wait to see you. <3

xo

***

Brian finished his deployment and quickly made his way home to me. Four weeks after he'd returned, we woke up on a Friday morning to the sound of his cell phone alarm chirping. I rolled over to kiss my husband good morning, and suddenly had that eerily familiar feeling of not feeling quite right. I kissed Brian on the forehead and Chance and I made our way downstairs to get some coffee and fresh air and wait for the feeling to pass while Brian got ready for work. The feeling of nausea wasn't passing and Brian came downstairs to find me curled up on our beige couch, Chance in my lap, glass bowl in my lap—just in case.

"Ughh, babe, I don't feel good, I think I've got the flu," I told him, a scowl forming on my face.

"Oh no, I'm sorry, babe. Can I get you some water? Want me to run to the store and get some medicine?" he asked, concerned, as he took a seat next to me on the couch. Chance growled and jumped down, highly offended that his position as my protector was now being overshadowed by Brian's presence.

"No, I'm OK, I think I just need to lay here for a little bit . . . maybe I'll drink some water. I don't really feel sick, just kind of naus—" I hadn't even finished the word nauseous before it hit me. *No way. Brian had only been home a month, was it possible?*

"What if I'm pregnant?" I looked up at Brian from my place on the couch, a smile forming on my lips as I began to think through the possibilities of it being true.

"What?" He coughed, caught off guard at my suggestion, but a slight smile quickly forming on his lips.

"It would be crazy, but crazier things have happened to us. This is the type of nausea I felt with Izzy. Babe." I started to laugh. We had talked about having another baby as soon as he got home from deployment and had taken no provisions to prevent ourselves from having one since he'd been home, so it was technically a possibility. "I'll get a test today and find out." I smiled at him as he grabbed my hand. "Oh boy . . ." He laughed, reaching my hand up to his lips to kiss it before winking and adding, "Just in case it's the flu."

Military families around the world can attest to the fact that family planning is a nice thought, but the reality of planning to have children is often scheduled between long deployments, travel, and everything else that comes up when your partner is called to duty. The reality is, you try as much and as often as you can while they're home (no complaints there) but are disappointed when you realize you didn't conceive and you're now saying goodbye to them, and your chance of having a baby, for another six months to a year, until they return home.

I called in sick to work for the day. I was nauseous and until I could confirm I wasn't infected with the flu, I thought I'd play it safe. I lay on the couch for the next hour, daydreaming about the possibility of having another baby with Brian. What if we had a boy? Or another girl, a sister for Izzy? Brian had previously warned me that submariners "only have girls." Izzy's nanny came to work for the day and I couldn't take it any longer, I got off the couch, and Chance and I drove down to our neighborhood Walgreens, the same one we had both driven to two years earlier to buy these same tests to find out we were having Izzy.

"Welcome to Walgreens, can I help you with anything?" I was greeted as I walked in.

"No thanks, I'm OK." This time around I knew where to go and what I was looking for. I found four tests—just in case—purchased them and drove home.

Positive.

+

Pregnant.

Positive.

Oh my gosh. I knew it! I waited patiently for Brian to come home from work to tell him the news. He barely had the door open before I was jumping in his arms. "We're having a baby!" I yelled, tears in my eyes, shoving one of the white sticks in his face to prove it—realizing after the fact that stick I was waving around had been previously dipped in my urine—but he didn't seem to mind; this was a moment to celebrate.

"No way! Are you serious?" Brian instantly had tears in his eyes as we hugged, standing in our kitchen hallway, reveling in the fact we were going to be parents again, and Izzy would soon have a sibling.

Eight weeks after finding out we were expecting baby Bugge number two, we were dropping Izzy off at my mom's house and headed to the airport to catch our red-eye flight to Sydney, Australia! I'd been slightly disappointed to realize I wouldn't be able to scuba dive on our epic scuba diving vacation, but I knew we'd still have an amazing time adventuring and exploring a new part of the world together, and it was a small price to pay to know we'd be expanding our family in a few months.

Australia was incredible and Fiji was just as exciting. Visiting iconic landmarks like the Sydney Opera House and driving across the Sydney Harbour Bridge—on the opposite side of the car and road—was a new experience for both Brian and me, and we laughed nervously as we each took turns driving throughout our trip. Despite our usual judgment, we were happy to have bought the extra car insurance as Brian navigated his way into a parking space at the wildlife sanctuary, commending himself on his expert parking skills despite being on the opposite side of the car, quite literally moments before backing into a tree—"It was just a tap!"—causing $1,200 worth of damage to the bumper of our rental car. We spent the rest our days in Australia and then Fiji holding hands, walking through the city, and driving out to the mountains. I bought a beach umbrella and a handful of books, and on diving days I relaxed on the beach as Brian dove these new waters, always anxious to get back to me and recount tales of what he'd just seen and how it was expanding his diving resume. "This is incredible, babe. I've been dreaming of scuba diving in Australia since I was ten years old and now it's coming true. This is unreal. I can't wait to dive the world." In that moment, I was proud of my husband, of us, for making each other's dreams come true and I had no doubt that we'd continue this lifestyle, and that he would in fact get to dive the world.

Chapter Twelve

"The results are supposed to come out this morning!" Brian said in a tone that conveyed just how anxious and excited he was. It was February 2016, and we were on FaceTime together while he was working in Hawaii, sitting in a back booth of the Waikiki IHOP restaurant, eyes glued to his computer screen waiting to see if he had made Limited Duty Officer (LDO). This was a promotion reserved for a select few service members in the Navy who didn't have a college degree, but had proven through their dedication, honor, courage, and commitment they were capable of leading the Navy to great places. It was a position offered to only six sailors in the entire US Navy this year and which took a presidential appointment to be offered to these individuals. Brian had been enlisted in the Navy for thirteen years and knew the odds were against him for being promoted into the elite LDO community. Peers of his had submitted packages year after year and not been picked up, so while he was confident in his unique skill set and leadership qualities, he was realistic with the fact he probably wouldn't be seeing his name appear on that list, no matter how many times he hit refresh.

Refresh.

Refresh.

"They'd be crazy not to offer it to you, babe," I tried reassuring him. I didn't want to put any pressure on him in the event his name wasn't on that list, but it was true, they'd be crazy to not offer it to him. Brian had proven himself to be the best of the best and I was hopeful the Navy would agree they saw in him what I did every single day.

"I mean, if I don't make it this year, I can try again next year. It's my first attempt so I shouldn't get my hopes up." I knew him well enough to know he was listening to himself talk rather than asking for a response. "But how cool would that be if I made it? This could potentially change everything for us."

"I know, babe." I tried not to laugh. He was nervous. I caught images of him biting his lower lip and running his fingers through his greasy hair as he alternated between our FaceTime screen and hitting refresh on the results page. He'd obviously woken up and headed straight down to the restaurant to await the results rather than take a shower, and his style of Christmas morning nervousness made me love him even more.

"Alright, I'm going to go and order my food. I'll call you as soon as I'm done babe, OK?"

We hung up and I turned my attention to Izzy, playing with her toy blocks at my feet. "Dadda's nervous, kiddo!" I said to myself more than her as I stood up to stretch, sore from baby number two residing in my belly. I arched my back and shrugged my shoulders before finding a place next to Izzy on the floor, just in time for my phone to chirp, indicating Brian was calling. *How come he's calling instead of FaceTime?*

"Hey, babe!" I said, smiling.

"Ash!" he said, loudly, firmly.

"What!? I shouted, startling Izzy and waking the sleeping baby in my belly.

"I made it. I freaking made LDO!" His voice boomed, full of pride. Separated by an ocean, from where he sat in this pancake restaurant to our home office in Gig Harbor, I could feel his pride. I could sense the light in his eyes, the smile on his face, as the gravity of this promotion began to sink in. He'd made it. In every sense of that phrase, he had made it.

"Shut up!!! Oh my gosh! Congratulations, sweetheart!" I said, beaming. We both started laughing. This was about to change everything. We had a lot of decisions to make from here, but the only thing that mattered in this moment was that his name was on that list—he'd made it.

UNCLASSIFIED//

R 251654Z FEB 16

FM CNO WASHINGTON DC

TO NAVADMIN

SUBJ/FY-17 ACTIVE-DUTY NAVY LIMITED DUTY OFFICER (LDO) AND CHIEF WARRANT

OFFICER (CWO) IN-SERVICE PROCUREMENT SELECTION BOARD RESULTS//

RMKS/1. Congratulations to selectees of the FY-17 Active-Duty Navy Limited
Duty Officer and Chief Warrant Officer In-service Procurement Board.

2. For LDO and CWO selectees, read name, commissioning month/year.
All appointments are effective on the first day of the commissioning month.
Members are directed to verify their select status via BUPERS Online.
Limited Duty Officer * Lieutenant (Junior Grade)

Bugge Brian James 0817

We spent the next few minutes on the phone with one another, rejoicing in what this meant for him as a sailor as well as for us as a family and talking through next steps. Brian would be commissioned in August 2017, so we were looking at waiting over a year for him to officially become an officer.

"Maybe now I can do a tour of shore duty," he mentioned toward the end of our conversation. "I've been out to sea for the past thirteen years, which truthfully is probably what prepared me for this promotion, but I'm tired of going to sea. I want to spend some time with you guys, work on school, diving, sailing. This will be a good opportunity for all of that. I'll talk to the detailer at work and see what our options are for duty stations once I commission."

He was excited. Hopeful. Proud. He'd worked hard for thirteen years to reach this monumental moment and I beamed while listening to him relish in the moment for what it was. "You ready to be an officer's wife?" he teased. *Indeed, I was.*

Upon his arrival home from his work trip, his command told him that they were going to create a position for him at his current duty station of Bangor, Washington.

"I imagine that you and Ashley have settled down here, you have another baby on the way, I think we could probably find a job to keep you here if you wanted to stay," his boss at work mentioned.

Brian hadn't considered getting to stay in the Pacific Northwest with this assignment, so he listened and nodded along, knowing it would be up to the Navy detailer to actually assign his next location, but he came home that night and explained they were going to push for him to get to stay here and take over for an exiting LDO. The truth was, it was still far too early to be making plans for any of this; he wouldn't be commissioning for another year and a half and anyone familiar with military life knows well enough that nothing is final, until it's final. And even then, there's a chance for change.

The initial shock soon began to wear off and we quickly fell back into our normal routine, which included the fact we were pregnant with baby number two and we'd soon be able to find out what we were having! Convinced that submariners only have girls, Brian and I were shocked and elated to find out we'd be having a baby boy. My pregnancy with baby number two was mostly—fortunately—uneventful. Brian was an attentive and nurturing partner, taking great care of me while pregnant, hoping to make up for the fact that he missed out on the first six months of our pregnancy with Izzy due to his being deployed. Friday evenings he'd come home with sweets or other pregnancy cravings and draw me a warm bath.

While Izzy slept upstairs, we'd sit on the couch holding hands, watching TV together and talking about what our lives were developing into and our goals for the future as a family of four. We spent these moments on the couch or in bed together trying to come up with the perfect name for our son, a much more challenging task than we'd anticipated. At one point, Brian and I had decided on the name Oliver; it was a cute young boy name, which translated well to a strong adult name too. We could picture ourselves yelling for Isabel and Oliver to come downstairs for dinner or to come inside after an afternoon of riding bikes down the street together. We loved it. We'd had that name in mind for nearly a month when we flew to San Francisco for my cousin Peter's wedding. At five months pregnant, we met up with my mother and my two aunts—the same ones who were present at the Irish coffee place after my grandmother's funeral, and who had yelled at Brian for paying—who all started asking about the pregnancy and if we'd picked out any names. Brian and I looked at each other before smiling and saying, "Oliver!" Without skipping a beat, the three matriarchs of my family belted in unison, "Awww, Olly!" And in that moment, with that simple nickname proclamation from the three of them, the name Oliver was no more. We didn't even need to discuss it; we gave each other a look that said, nope, absolutely not, and mentally scratched that name off the list: ~~Oliver.~~ Back to square one.

Eventually, we settled on the name Hudson Belmont Bugge, which sounded polished and regal to us. Hudson has been a name I've liked for as long as I can remember and Belmont is a neighborhood in Portland, Oregon, near and dear to our hearts, where Brian and I spent a lot of our time together while dating in the early years, eating lunch at Pad Thai or playing Skee-Ball at the Wonderland nickel arcade. As we'd done with baby Isabel, we wanted to keep his middle name something with significant meaning to us as a couple and now as a family.

As baby Hudson continued growing inside of me, Brian and I spent as much time out on *Time and Tide* as we could, taking Izzy for sunset cruises and anchoring out to watch the harbor seals play. We slowly started to have engine issues with her, and with as much time as we spent on the water we knew we needed to get it looked at. We called Tom, a local diesel mechanic who holds a striking resemblance to Duckie from the movie *Pretty in Pink*, who was the bearer of bad news when he told us it would cost more to fix the engine than the boat was worth. Brian and I looked at each other and we instantly knew what our next adventure was going to consist of: operation finding a new sailboat.

Easier said than done. We had to find something reliable, comfortable, big enough for a family of four—and growing—and that could perform well in races, something Brian had been wanting to get into. The first sailboat we looked at which met all of our wants and needs was a 1975 Morgan three-quarter-ton, thirty-six-foot IOR boat named *Goldilocks*. She had a brand-new engine, a tiller, adequate space below for our family, an extensive sail inventory, and . . . was bright golden-yellow. Yellow. A yellow sailboat. I couldn't shield my eyes from it. I had no words. A yellow sailboat named *Goldilocks* with three bears painted on her hull. No way. We looked around, we asked what the price was—dang, we could afford her—but she was yellow. We went back to the drawing board, searching for a boat that had everything *Goldilocks* had, that was within our budget, but that wasn't bright yellow. We continued searching, knowing we wouldn't be Brian and Ashley, the Bugges, without a sailboat in our family. We needed to be out on the water so we searched. And searched. And searched. Nothing compared to *Goldilocks*.

"But she's just *so* yellow," I said to Brian, knowing it didn't matter. In all of her yellow glory, she was the boat for us, and she was going to be ours.

"I know, but . . ." That dimple told me all I needed to know. Brian called the sailboat broker soon after this conversation and we were quickly making plans to sign the loan paperwork and bring her home.

We hoisted *Goldilocks*'s mainsail for the first time March 17, 2016, on her maiden voyage to her new home port of Gig Harbor, Washington, on a bright, beautiful, and blue-sky-filled April afternoon. We set sail with a course heading toward Mount Rainier, past sweeping views of the Seattle skyline, through the channels and buoy markers we'd sailed a hundred times prior, and while these waters of the Puget Sound were familiar, this time was different. We were now on our new-to-us sailboat, our very yellow new-to-us sailboat, and we were bringing her home.

"How much do you think it would cost to paint her?" I asked from my place at the tiller as Brian tidied the lines.

Brian looked at me as a slight smile crept up from the corner of his lips. He already knew the answer to this question. Dang it, that wasn't a good sign.

"I'd say $12,000," he mouthed, turning his head into the wind as if that would save him from the look of shock that quickly overtook my face.

"I'm sorry, what?" I'd heard what he had said. I just didn't want to believe it. Between the wind, the sun, and his place in the companionway, it was possible I had misunderstood him.

"I said, $12,000." He laughed. That boyish grin he knew I couldn't possibly get upset with was spreading across his face. He knew it was way out of our budget as he said it.

"So, I guess she's going to stay gold?" I laughed. It was what it was. And that was a very golden-yellow sailboat.

"Yeah, she's probably going to stay gold," Brian said.

We knew we didn't want to keep the name *Goldilocks*, but we'd been throwing around name ideas for the few days prior and hadn't come up with anything spectacular, yet as soon as he said the words *Stay Gold*, something inside of us clicked. Stay Gold was the name of a punk band I had grown up listening to and was also the theme of Brian's favorite Robert Frost poem, "Nothing Gold Can Stay."

It was perfect. It meant something different to each of us, but we had come up with it together and it was perfect. *Stay Gold* was now ours.

A few days later, with *Stay Gold* safe in her slip, Brian came home from work looking concerned. I knew him well enough to tell he was trying to come up with the courage to tell me something. Bad news? Good news? Another deployment?

"You OK, babe?" I asked.

"Well . . ." he began, "work was interesting today . . . I have some news."

"Oh no . . . another deployment? When?" I braced myself.

"Ha ha, no, not exactly a deployment. More of a permanent change of station . . ." he finally said.

"What do you mean?" I asked, not quite sure what he was telling me. Was this good news or bad news? Would he be home for the birth of our son? The thoughts started racing through my head before he interrupted them.

"How do you feel about moving to Hawaii?" he asked, looking me in the eyes to gauge my reaction.

"Huh?" I coughed, my six-months-pregnant belly and I caught off guard with his question.

"I talked to the detailer today at work and he said we can't stay here. I've been in the Northwest too long and he thinks I will get burned out if I stay on sea duty any longer, so basically, we need to move." It was that simple. Pawns in a game of Navy chess, we were being picked up and moved to another location in our first Permanent Change of Station (PCS) move after an entire career served in the Pacific Northwest.

"Wait, what?" I asked. "I thought we told your work we didn't want to move, what happened?" I knew better than to pretend we had any kind of control over our military life. But I just felt like I needed a moment to process what he was saying to me.

"I know, but then I talked to the detailer and he more or less said we couldn't stay here. I've been here too long, and I need the opportunity at professional development in another setting. This doesn't mean we can't come back here after this next tour, there will always be opportunities for me here." There was a pitch in his voice that gave away how excited he was about what he was telling me and I tried my best to wrap my head around what he was saying. *We weren't staying in the Northwest? We were moving? When? Wait, did he say Hawaii in there somewhere?*

"Wait, did you say Hawaii?! Babe, did you say we're moving to Hawaii!?" I looked up suddenly, realizing what he had just said. *Hawaii!?* Hawaii had quickly become our home away from home during the past year while he'd spent so much time working there and we knew we loved it. We'd spent hours talking about the possibility of living there someday, enjoying afternoons together on the beach, teaching our kids to surf and swim in the tropical warm waters and eating fresh fruit picked from our own yard.

"I know I should have talked to you first, but I figured this is what you'd say. I talked to the detailer this morning and asked him to put our name on the list for it. We're penciled in for Hawaii in August 2017 after I commission. Of course, things can change, but for now, yep, we're moving to Hawaii." He laughed as I jumped into his arms, Chance suddenly growling on the couch next to me, upset that I'd disturbed his sleep with my commotion.

"Oh my god, but we just bought the boat," I said. "A yellow boat!!" Now laughing, thinking about having to put the yellow boat we'd just purchased up for sale. *Who was going to buy a yellow sailboat?*

"I know," Brian said in the sweetest tone, trying to calm me down. "There is nothing I can do about the orders to move, but we'll figure everything else out as we go along, OK?"

We knew we wouldn't be able to sell *Stay Gold*, nor did we really want to, and we knew it would be too expensive to hire somebody to sail it to Hawaii for us, so instead, Brian and I came up with a crazy solution: Brian would sail it across the Pacific and all the way to our new destination of Honolulu, Hawaii. Since first learning to sail years earlier, he'd dreamed of completing a transpacific crossing and this was his opportunity. He had the boat, the desire, and the knowledge as well as a supportive wife who encouraged him to chase after his dreams; barring something crazy happening, he was going to do it. We just had a few hurdles to get through first, including the birth of our son.

Baby Hudson was ready to join our family. This time around, we actually made it on time to the hospital—the same one where I had delivered Isabel—but they forgot about us. We spent over an hour in the room, waiting for my nurse to come and get me ready for what was about to happen. Brian and I didn't mind the quiet time one bit. We spent it talking about our plans for the future and savoring the magical moments we were living: a flourishing marriage, a beautiful family, great careers, and a year full of adventure just ahead of us. We had made it.

I labored for sixteen hours and it was a hard delivery. I felt nauseous but I didn't throw up this time—fool me once, minestrone. Brian was by my side the entire time, holding my hand.

"You're incredible, sweetheart, you've got this," I heard Brian whisper in my ear as I labored and eventually delivered Hudson into the world. I relied on his support and focused on his touch, his warmth, and his sweet words.

Hudson Belmont Bugge, our beautiful and healthy baby boy, was born June 1, 2016, weighing six pounds, fifteen ounces. Brian cut the umbilical cord, and then they placed the baby on my chest, a magical moment I had loved with Isabel and made sure to cherish with Hudson. I looked at him and I knew from that moment on that this guy would have my heart for the rest of my life.

Chapter Thirteen

Hudson was born on a Wednesday. We were home Thursday and back into our hectic routine by Saturday. Chance took to baby Hudson quickly, offering him wet-nosed kisses and curious nudges, while Hudson's two-year-old big sister, Isabel, was not as interested. Not even curious. Quite the opposite, in fact. Izzy would go out of her way to avoid looking at him, she certainly wasn't interested in acknowledging him, and holding him was absolutely out of the question. As far as Izzy was concerned, she was still an only child and if she protested hard enough, this foreign object currently taking up space in our house would soon find its way back to where it came from.

It took a few weeks, but she eventually came around and began interacting with her new baby brother, just in time for us to begin thinking about getting our new family of four, and our yellow sailboat, to Hawaii. We had over a year to prepare ourselves, much more than a typical military family preparing for a permanent change of station (PCS) move. With this luxury of time, we had the ability to plan our move, but also the worry that the Navy would be changing Brian's orders for another duty station, or any other number of changes that you learn to expect when part of the military. We began looking into our options for getting *Stay Gold* to Hawaii and were quickly confronted with the reality that sailing your thirty-six-foot boat across an ocean wasn't a typical PCS move tactic, and there was very little information on how to make this happen, with support of the Navy.

Early on Brian and I had established ourselves as a couple that wasn't afraid of the unknown; we knew the best rewards were those we worked hard for and this would be no different. Brian had openly daydreamed about wanting to sail a boat across an ocean someday, and as we began to consider how we would get *Stay Gold* to Hawaii, this daydream suddenly began turning into a tangible goal.

"What if I sailed her?" he asked one afternoon as we sailed through the deep blue waters of the Tacoma Narrows on a particularly sunny day.

"Sail her . . . as in from Washington to Hawaii?" I looked up from my place in the companionway where I was feeding baby Hudson a bottle and keeping my eye on Izzy as she played with the winch handles on the floor of the cabin below.

"Yeah . . . is that crazy?" he asked, looking to me for a reaction letting him know it was a terrible idea and we'd need to figure something else out, or the reassurance that it wasn't such a crazy idea after all.

I trusted Brian and his sailing skills implicitly, but we were both aware that sailing across the Pacific was a massive undertaking and was not the same as spending a weekend sailing around the relatively calm waters of the Puget Sound. That being said, the way he asked if it was crazy let me know he needed my support and confidence, not a list of reasons why it was dangerous.

"No, it's not crazy. That would be the adventure of a lifetime, babe! I think that would be freaking awesome," I responded, knowing he would latch on to those words and see it now as a possibility instead of an unattainable idea floating around in his head. From this moment moving forward, the idea was out there and we spent the next year of our lives making decisions and putting things in place to make this dream come true for him.

Step one: log more hours on *Stay Gold.*

Step two: put together a crew.

We had talked about the possibility of me going along on the crossing, but with two small children at home, an impending move immediately after sailing, and still needing to work full-time through it all, we decided it was best for me to sit this one out, instead coordinating efforts from the safety of our home office. Truthfully, in the back of our heads we were worried something could potentially happen out there in the open ocean and we wanted to make sure one of us was safe to raise the kids in that event. With this in mind, Brian started looking for people interested in joining his crew for local sailing races around the Sound. We entered *Stay Gold* in Wednesday-night beer can races and longer buoy races to get accustomed to handling *Stay Gold* in varying degrees of weather, fine-tuning sail trim, changing out the headsail in less than desirable conditions, climbing the mast for a lost halyard while underway. These were all skills that needed to be practiced and perfected before heading out into the open ocean, but the biggest learning curve was making decisions as the captain of his boat, drawing on his experience as a leader in the Navy and communicating his decisions effectively to his crew. Brian used his savvy technology skills to put together a website for *Stay Gold*, advertising crew positions for different races and blogging about his journey in getting *Stay Gold* ready for a transpacific crossing. People began taking interest in what he was doing, and soon *Stay Gold* had a decent-sized social media following, as well as the support of our community, who recognized her by her bright gold hull and sails as we left our slip, heading out of the safety of our harbor for a day of sailing.

Brian's confidence grew with every hour, every day, every race he logged on *Stay Gold* and soon he was ready to push himself further, the ultimate goal of getting her to Hawaii becoming a clear reality now within reach.

"I think I'm going to enter the Oregon Offshore race," he told me one day, after coming home from one of his many afternoons spent on *Stay Gold.*

"What's that?" I asked, intrigued by the excitement in his voice.

"It's a three-day-long race," he explained. "You sail from Astoria, Oregon, to Victoria, British Columbia, in Canada. Would you want to do it with me? I'm going to ask the rest of the crew too."

"Hmmm." I smiled at him. "Maybe? When is it?"

"Well, that's the thing . . . it's over Mother's Day weekend. But I was thinking we could ask one of our moms to hang out with Izzy and Hudson and you could do the race with me and we could celebrate Mother's Day when we arrive in Canada." He was excited. I could tell by the inflection in his voice he'd already put a lot of thought into this and how he could manage to do the race while still making me feel special for Mother's Day.

"Oh . . ." I was taken aback. He had always made an incredible effort to make me feel loved on every holiday we had together; this wasn't typical of him to plan something that would impede on such a special day. I thought about it for a moment, realizing quickly it would be selfish of me to make him feel anything other than excited about the opportunity to compete in a race like this, and he had obviously already put effort into my feelings and how he could manage both.

"Well, I want to spent Mother's Day with the kids, so what if you do the race, enjoy it, kick its butt, and the kids and I will meet you at the finish line in Canada?" I asked, more talking out loud than making a solid plan.

I hadn't even finished my thought as Brian walked over to me, wrapped his arms around me, and looked me in the eyes as he said, "How in the world did I get so lucky? You're the best thing that's ever happened to me, you know that, right? I don't know what I did, but I will spend the rest of my life making sure you know how thankful I am for you and the way you support me."

Stay Gold was soon registered for the race, and Brian was in full prep mode. He'd go to work all day, come home, eat dinner with the kids and me, and then head down to the boat until late into the evening, doing his best to juggle work and family life with the attention *Stay Gold* required. There was minor repair work to be done. He needed to spend time with his crew practicing maneuvers and man-overboard drills. There were safety-at-sea seminars to attend, first aid classes, specific specs the race required, which needed to be fixed and replaced on the boat, and it all took time, energy, and the undivided attention of Brian.

"Do you feel ready for it?" I asked as race day suddenly appeared within sight on our joint calendar. I believed in him. I just wanted to make sure he believed in himself.

"I'll know after the delivery. Getting *Stay Gold* down to Astoria and through the Columbia River Bar will either make or break my confidence and there's no turning back from there, so we'll see." He was half joking, but in all reality, I understood the significance of his crossing the bar. Affectionately referred to as the graveyard of the Pacific, it's a treacherous stretch of the Northwest coast, connecting the mighty Columbia River to the Pacific Ocean; with its tidal rips and unpredictable weather, this specific stretch of sand and water has brought down over two thousand ships and countless lives. It takes a very capable captain and crew as well as the right weather conditions, perhaps a little bit of luck, and a whole lot of guts to make that initial turn into the current.

Over the next few days, the plans we'd been making came to fruition: Brian and the crew sailed *Stay Gold* down to Astoria, successfully crossing the bar for the first time, and the kids and I were there to meet him. We spent the next couple of days getting the boat ready for the race, buying water and provisions, attending the kick-off dinner to meet the other competitors, checking tides and wind patterns, and strategizing about how to get past the starting buoy and not let up until *Stay Gold* and crew reached Canada. Just like that, it was Go Time! I kissed Brian and we waved *Stay Gold* a bon voyage as she left the safety of her slip in Astoria and headed back for her second Columbia River Bar crossing in just as many days. I spent the next forty-eight hours tracking *Stay Gold* via our GPS race tracker, watching as she'd tack and jibe, catching pockets of wind and weather, taking the lead and then falling back in her class of competitors, making her way up the Oregon and Washington coasts. Brian sent me photos and text messages as he was able to, updating me on what they were eating, how big the waves were—at one point there was talk of sixteen-foot swells—and how morale on the boat was. I watched online as other racers fell back, or out of the race completely, but *Stay Gold* and crew held their own and charged toward Canadian waters. Three days after we had said our goodbye in Astoria, I loaded Izzy, Hudson, and my mom, who was visiting for Mother's Day, in Brian's beloved black Subaru and drove toward Port Angeles to catch the ferry, which would take us to Canada to celebrate *Stay Gold* and her fourth place finish in her first large-scale sailing race.

The Oregon Offshore race proved to be the biggest learning curve for Brian. He'd always been an incredibly humble man and took things to heart, beating himself up about things he thought he should have done or been capable of doing better.

"You OK, babe?" I asked him. I could tell there was something that was weighing heavily on his mind. He and a friend from the Navy had sailed the boat home from Victoria after the race and he was now sitting on the couch, elbows on his kneecaps, head lowered between his hands as he ran his fingers through his light brown hair.

"Ash," he said, taking a deep sigh that felt desperate. "I don't think I'm ready for the TransPac."

"Why do you say that?" I asked, sitting next to him, putting my arm around him and hearing the serious doubt in his voice.

"Because I barely made it through these three days. The TransPac is coming up so quickly and it will take at least three weeks." I was looking for that dimple, but it wasn't there. His eyes told me he was seriously rethinking what he had been working so hard for. "It's just that so many things went wrong in these three days . . . the engine died, we didn't have enough provisions, we didn't have our shifts worked out. I feel like I failed my crew as their captain . . ." He ran his fingers through his hair, then he looked up, sighed deeply, and said, "I have spent so much time away from you and the kids on getting this boat ready, and I still wasn't prepared. How am I going to make it to Hawaii?" I hugged my arm around him tighter, knowing at this point, he just needed me to listen to him. "At one point, I'm going to be 1,500 miles from anything, anyone, and anywhere. If anything happens out there to me, or the crew, or the boat, we're on our own. The Coast Guard only goes 500 miles offshore, so what if someone gets hurt, or we lose the rig? We'd have to hope a shipping vessel would see us and help out. It's one thing if it's just me, but after these past three days at sea, it's sinking in that I'm going to be responsible for these guys out there. I just don't want to let them down."

I could tell the offshore race had him questioning his abilities, not as a sailor, but as a captain. It pained me to see him waning in the knowledge, experience, and confidence I knew he had inside of him. He felt the responsibility of being in charge of an expedition that could go wrong. He didn't want to disappoint me, the kids, or anybody who was relying on him. His voice, his words, his body language, the way he was looking at me from his place under my arm on the couch, I knew this was a make-or-break moment. This moment was going to decide whether he would summon the courage to continue working toward this lifelong dream of his, or if he'd let it go. He was looking to me for guidance. It would have been easy to tell him that he'll get another chance at some point in his life, that he could take some time to think about it, that we could buy another boat in Hawaii and maybe he could sail that one to our next destination, that there were any number of excuses or outs he could use to get out of having to do this … But that wasn't me. It wasn't Brian. And it certainly wasn't us. We didn't live our lives with sentences that begin with "Maybe one day . . ." We believed in the here and now, in making the moments count. And most of all, I believed in him. I knew he could do it and he needed to know that.

"Babe, listen to me," I began, taking my arm from around his shoulder and reaching for his hand. "You can do this, I know you can." I looked into his deep blue eyes, connecting with him as I said, "Whatever happened during the Oregon Offshore, you need to take from it, learn from it, and then shake it off. You know this boat better than anyone and you're absolutely capable of doing this journey. It's three weeks of time that will change your entire life. Think of how accomplished you will feel when you set foot on land for the first time after crossing an ocean in your sailboat." Brian had tears in his eyes as he grasped my hand tighter, soaking up the words I was saying to him. I was giving him a gift he couldn't give himself in the moment, the confidence needed to see this journey through. I knew he valued what I was saying, so I continued on, "Your crew is going to look to you for guidance. They're going to feed off of your energy, your experience, and your ability to communicate with them. You're all going to have down days out there, this journey is going to change each of you, but you are the most competent and capable captain of *Stay Gold* and you need to be able to see that before you set sail. I know you can do it, and when you're in the middle of the ocean, 1,500 miles from land in any direction, you come back to this conversation and know that I am here, supporting you and cheering you on, OK?"

"OK." A modest smile appeared on his face, and with it, the slightest glimpse of that left cheek dimple.

"What do we need to do to make you feel more confident? To get you ready for this trip?" I asked as I left the room, in search of pen and paper to begin making a list. I found what I was looking for and returned to the living room, this time sitting on the floor in front of the coffee table scribbling TRANSPAC in bold letters across the yellow pad of paper, and looked up at Brian, still on the couch, before saying, "Alright, let's figure this out. What do we need to buy? What projects need to get done on the boat? What will make you feel safe out there?"

He looked at me with so much love. His eyes, filled with sadness a minute ago, were now regaining their lively, passionate spark: the spark which I'd fallen in love with, had come to know in my life as what it felt like to be in love with the man of my dreams, the spark that ignited my own desire to accomplish incredible things. In that moment, I knew I had him back. I sat on the floor in front of the coffee table, savoring the moment for what it was—a shift in our relationship, a tangible moment of time that we would look back on and know we could and would truly support one another through everything—as he took a deep breath and began listing everything we needed to get himself, the boat, and our family ready for this undertaking.

From that day forward, Brian and *Stay Gold* became one. He spent every waking hour he wasn't at work, or on travel for work, down at the marina, working on getting her ready. The Oregon Offshore had been a good shakedown cruise to test her seaworthiness, and with the exception of a few small leaks and other minor issues, she had done well and was ready for the journey. It was Brian that needed to prepare himself, physically, mentally, and psychologically. He began buying items to outfit the boat, using the motto "Two is one and one is none" every time I scoffed at our credit card statement and the amount of times "West Marine Purchase" appeared on it. He had my full support in this endeavor, but this process didn't come cheap and we ended up spending nearly $20,000 on getting *Stay Gold* ready for the three-week TransPac, more than we had initially paid for her. But seeing Brian's excitement, knowing this would be the journey of a lifetime, was truly invaluable. We used our savings and credit cards and even started a fund-raiser to help with the efforts, offering afternoon sails and crew gear for donations to put toward the purchase of a satellite phone, EPIRB, new lines, sail repair kits, and fuel. You name it and there was a cost associated with it, and we had to come up with it somehow. In all actuality, Brian had started utilizing social media to promote what he was doing, and we had picked up some traction with our local community as people started to take notice that he was down working on her day after day, night after night. The news began buzzing around town and pretty soon it began crossing borders, with people paying attention to what Brian and his crew were getting ready to do. A tattooed Navy guy with a wife and two young children getting ready to PCS from Washington to Hawaii on a thirty-six-foot yellow sailboat. It doesn't happen every day. The mission in itself was fascinating, obviously. It had that aura of an all-American adventure, the story of a man and his love of the sea, setting out on a grand expedition into the great unknown with the potential for danger.

As the departure date approached, more and more people would show up at the marina to catch a glimpse of the yellow sailboat and the thirty-three-year-old captain who would soon be heading out on the adventure of a lifetime. People wanted to be a part of it, they wanted a taste of that adventure, even if it meant just standing there, soaking in the sun, feeling like they were sending a part of themselves on this journey across the Pacific with Brian.

Word of Brian's undertaking circulated through town enough that soon we had press reaching out to us, wanting to interview Brian, to find out more about his experience, who he was as a sailor, a captain, a husband and father, a member of the military. They were anxious to learn more about the journey itself, the logistics that would go into making the trip possible and his inspiration for making this happen. At one point we were even approached by a local marine supply store who offered *Stay Gold* a sponsorship; we'd advertise for them and they'd give us a discount on the boating supplies we were already buying there. Deal. Sign us up. It was truly an incredible and humbling experience.

"What's happening!?" Brian laughed as he finished reading another email, this time from a reporter with the *Military Times* magazine interested in covering his unusual PCS story.

"Babe, I don't think you realize how excited people are about what you're doing. Nobody does stuff like this! People dream of doing this, but nobody actually does it. You're making it happen, people want to grab onto that!" I smiled proudly at my handsome husband. He was literally making his dreams come true and it was inspirational to be a part of. One minute we're buying a yellow sailboat with three ugly bears on the hull and the next we're getting ready for the adventure of a lifetime, with sponsors and reporters and a community of people cheering us on. Surreal.

Brian had done hours of research on tides, wind and weather patterns, and a number of other variables—including the only available three weeks in his and his crew's schedule—and come up with a departure date of July 6, 2017. With the crew scheduled to arrive beginning July 2, this gave us a few final days to get everything put together before their arrival. With Izzy and Hudson at home with their nanny, I was down on the boat putting some groceries away with Brian topside when I heard voices on the dock.

"Wow, I heard about your journey. I would have loved to do something like this when I was younger." I looked out the port-side window to see an older gentleman approaching Brian, extending his hand and obviously eager to talk to Brian.

"Hey," Brian said, "I put my pants on one leg at a time just like everybody else."

The gentleman smiled and started asking Brian about his naval service, and the route he'd be taking, if he'd be making any stops, how much water he'd have on board. Brian answered all of his questions, the excitement apparent in his voice as he said, "It's never too late. If I can do it, you can do it. This has been my dream for so long, I just never really thought it would be possible until this opportunity came up and my wife told me to go for it!"

That man looked at Brian in awe, trying to absorb as much of Brian's motivation and zest for life as he possibly could. I eaves-dropped from my place in the cabin a few moments longer before appearing topside, Brian smiling at the sight of me appearing, extending his hand to help me out of the companionway to where he was standing. People were aware he had a wife and two children who were supporting him on this adventure, and this contributed to the fascination that people felt toward Brian and the *Stay Gold* crew.

"Don't give up on your dream. If you want to do it, you can," Brian said, placing his arm around me and turning toward the man again. "All you need to do is make a plan, find yourself a hot wife who'll support you, and go for it!"

We all laughed, the man thanked Brian for his time and service, as well as mine, before shaking our hands and walking away.

As the days leading up to July 6 quickly passed, the crew arrived in town, hundreds of gallons of water and sunscreen were purchased, rum and other provisions were brought on board, and the final preparations for *Stay Gold*'s departure were put in place. The crew consisted of Chris, whom we met through the local sailing community and was an expert navigator; Willy, a childhood friend with years of sailing experience and who also just happened to be on a brief hiatus from touring with his band; and my cousin Beau, a middle school teacher with no sailing experience to speak of, but who had summers off and—much like Brian—couldn't say no to the opportunity of adventure. This was a solid crew of men, each bringing their own set of skills, some in sailing, some in leadership, some in personality, but all with a desire to do something great. They were about to get their chance.

The morning of July 6, 2017, was spent running around the house, making a final dash to the store for last-minute items—and doughnuts—and meeting the entire crew down at the boat for the bon voyage party I'd arranged. Our local newspaper had run an article on *Stay Gold* and advertised the opportunity to come down to the public dock for the send-off and to wish her crew fair winds and following seas. As you walked toward the end of the dock, *Stay Gold* stood out in all her yellow glory against a backdrop of the beautiful calm deep blue waters of Gig Harbor. Sounds from the DJ we'd hired bounced around among a sea of blue and white balloons, reporters and photographers, sailors in uniform who had come down from the submarine base to see Brian off, and lots of friends and family members wearing dark blue T-shirts and hats with *Stay Gold* printed across the front in gold lettering. Our sailboat had become such a symbol of Gig Harbor during the few months leading up to this, and it was heartwarming to see so many members of our community on our dock this morning, all wanting to shake hands with this brave young man about to take on this incredible voyage. Brian had planned for a 10 a.m. push time and as the clock started winding down, he stepped off the boat, grabbed the microphone from the DJ, cleared his voice, and held Hudson in his arms as he said to the crowd who had gathered, "This is the crew that is going to take the boat 2,300 nautical miles to Honolulu from here. We leave in twenty-nine minutes, but it's taken us a year and a half to get to this point and there are many people standing right here who have made that happen." He then looked around, meeting each person's gaze, and added, "I just want to say thank you. Thank you very much for taking time out of your day to come down here and see us off. It really means a lot to everybody." Then, he raised a glass and said, "Cheers!" And everybody followed him in unison: "Cheers, and stay gold!"

Isabel, who was dressed in her favorite navy blue shirt, stole the crowd's attention as she took the microphone and with her sweet little two-year-old voice said, "Hi Dada, I love you so much!" before she leapt into the arms of her beaming dad. From my place next to Brian on the dock and in my own *Stay Gold* navy sweat-shirt, I took my turn at well wishes into the microphone: "Congrat-ulations to all of you guys, I hope you have a great time. Take lots of pictures and I can't wait to see you in Hawaii." Then I looked at Brian and his crew and said, "Enjoy it. Enjoy every minute of it."

Brian shook hands and gave hugs to those closest to him on the dock, giving Izzy and Hudson a special moment each to tell them he loved them, and then pulled me aside for a semi-private embrace and to tell me in a shared moment only the two of us will ever understand the emotion behind: "I wish you were coming with me. I know I'm the one sailing, but you're the reason this is happening and this dream of mine wouldn't be a reality without you. I don't know if I'll ever have the words to tell you how much you mean to me, but thank you. I love you so much, Ash." We hugged, we kissed, and with a crowd of people watching, he hopped on board to join his crew, blowing the air horn to signify their departure, and just like that, they were underway. Izzy waved goodbye from my arms, shouting "I want to go on the boat with Dada!" as I smiled, overcome with a powerful sense of pride in this wonderful man I had married. We'd used Brian's weather calculations to determine it would take them anywhere from sixteen to twenty-four days to sail over, and we'd be able to use our GPS tracker onboard to monitor their progress, so we bought tickets to arrive on Oahu eighteen days later and hope we'd be there in time to watch *Stay Gold* arrive in her new port, greeting the love of my life with cold beer, hot kisses, and a whole lot of aloha.

Chapter Fourteen

"Land ho!" Brian yelled through the cell phone clutched tightly in his hand. "We're close!" I couldn't see her golden hull cutting through the bright blue Hawaiian waters yet, but I could feel her presence, and that of her handsome captain, and I knew *Stay Gold* was close. I beamed into my phone receiver.

"We're headed into Pearl Harbor now, you should see us in the next few minutes! I need a cold beer and a hot shower but I can't wait to wrap my arms around you. Full disclosure, babe, I stink." Brian's voice was an odd mix of triumph, loneliness, exhaustion, and excitement. I stood on the end of the pier, next to our family and friends who had flown in for the occasion, all eyes straining the horizon for the first sight of her, until finally, the slightest outline of a sailboat, a yellow sailboat, making her way home. Twenty minutes later, as the warm Hawaiian sun began to rise over the tops of our heads, I beamed with pride as *Stay Gold* and crew were suddenly in front of us. Brian threw me the docking lines to tie off as he hopped over the lifelines, setting foot on dry land for the first time in twenty-one days, running past the outstretched arms awaiting him in order to run toward me, immediately planting a well-deserved and much-needed kiss on my lips as friends from around the world commented and applauded via Facebook livestream. Brian had done it. He had successfully sailed our thirty-six-foot sailboat from Washington to Hawaii, and in the process achieved a life dream of his. The four-man crew emerged from their places on the weather-beaten boat, sunburned, faces full of stubble, and looking slightly trimmer than when we had last seen them.

"Holy crap. We made it." Beau kicked off the remarks, which sent the four men into a bout of laughter only they would understand the depths of. We watched in awe as these men all took a moment to look at one another, smile, hug, clink cold beer cans together, and say cheers to *Stay Gold.*

They'd have stories to share with their family and friends over Thanksgiving dinner for years to come, but when they closed their eyes and thought back to their journey across the Pacific, only those four men would know what it felt like, what it tasted like, what it meant.

After securing *Stay Gold* in her new slip, Brian and I took a moment together away from the chorus of alohas happening around us, and he wrapped his arms around me.

"I want to hear all about it!. What did it feel like? What was the best part? Worst part? How did everyone get along? How do you feel now that it's over?" I had a thousand questions for him. It's important to note, he wasn't wrong, he did smell. Not of the salt water, fresh air, and new beginnings you'd picture in a moment like this, but of three weeks' worth of sweat, diesel fuel, and dried sunscreen. I didn't mind.

"I kept a journal while sailing," he told me as we walked hand in hand toward the arrival party I'd arranged. "I wanted to capture all that we went through, but I'm not sure my words could even do that. I want you to read it."

"I'd love to." I smiled and squeezed his hand. Brian had a way with words and I knew this journal would be raw and honest and I couldn't wait to experience the trip through his eyes. "Maybe on the flight home?" he suggested. We had just arrived in Hawaii, but we'd soon have to fly back to Washington. Brian was going to be commissioned as an officer in the Navy and right after the ceremony he'd be flying to Rhode Island for training while the kids and I packed up the house and moved. We had a busy few weeks ahead of us, but for now all that mattered was Brian had just crossed an ocean in our sailboat and we needed to celebrate this accomplishment. We enjoyed our next few days in Hawaii together, sipping mai tais at the beachfront bar in front of our hotel and watching Izzy and Hudson splash in the salty surf before it was time to fly home for our last few days as residents of Washington State.

On August 1, 2017, with the sun shining brightly outside of the Bangor Navy Chapel, Brian James Bugge, at the age of thirty-five, was adorned with two ensign bars on either side of his chest, becoming part of the elite group of Limited Duty Officers in the US Navy. During our years together, I'd seen him in many hats, both physically and metaphorically, but throughout all of his Navy ceremonies, I'd never seen him look prouder than this moment as he recited his oath of office and three-year-old Izzy placed his new khaki LDO cover on his head. The Navy band played, colors were presented, and Brian's best friend, Nick, gave an impassioned speech recalling their years as lowly sailors working their way up in the Navy together, "Never forget" being their motto during those early years.

"Never forget how freaking terrible this is and that we don't want to re-enlist when the time comes!" Nick laughed, pride in his voice for what Brian had accomplished since those sentiments had been exchanged in the hallways of their first submarine, the USS *Pennsylvania*. No matter how hard it had been, Nick and Brian had banded together in those early years and both now had their eyes set on Navy retirement in the not-so-distant future.

"Next up will be the first salute." Brian's master of ceremony explained to all of us watching from the audience. He went on to explain, "When a previously enlisted sailor is commissioned as an officer in the Navy, tradition calls for the Ensign to buy their first salute from somebody who has helped mentor them or offered special support to get them to this place in their career. We say the candidate buys the first salute using a silver dollar—while the other ones are earned." The candidate can choose the person, and to nobody's surprise Brian chose Uncle Mike, who had served as a friend and mentor throughout the years, and who was now preparing to offer his friend and former roommate the most meaningful salute of his career. We all knew this was a special moment as Brian and Uncle Mike stood on stage facing one another, and with the exception of the clicking sound of our hired photographer, the chapel was silent in anticipation. Uncle Mike brought his hand up to salute, Brian followed suit. I stood from my place in the front pew with tears in my eyes as I witnessed this exchange, unbelievably proud of Brian and incredibly thankful for Uncle Mike and the role he'd played in our lives, including this monumental moment.

They both look so handsome in their uniforms. I wonder if the caterers will know where to set up the food at the reception. Don't forget to grab Hudson's shoes from the car . . .

I was lost in thought when I realized an uncomfortable amount of time had passed and they were still standing facing one another, both with hands still in salute position. Uncle Mike whispered something to Brian under his breath. Brian whispered something back. There were eyebrows raised between the two, questioning glances, and hands moved quickly and awkwardly. I knew both of them well enough to know what was happening, and before I knew it I was laughing. They stood there holding that pose, on stage, in front of everyone, trying to figure out who was supposed to drop the salute first. According to tradition, Uncle Mike should have saluted Brian first, as a way to show respect to him for the newly earned title. However, Brian saluted him first, and those who saw what had happened snickered from their place in the crowd.

Ten days after completing his transpacific sailing voyage and six days after commissioning as an officer in the Navy, Brian left the Pacific Northwest for the last time, flying to Rhode Island for officer training school while the kids and I packed up our home in Washington and flew back to begin our new life in Hawaii.

Isabel, Hudson, Chance, and I spent our first few weeks on the island exploring the white sand beaches, scouting out the best Hawaiian shaved ice stands, playing in the hotel pool, and counting down the days until Brian would be joining us. Finally, September 15, 2017, on a bright and warm Friday afternoon, I hopped in our black Subaru, now adorned with Hawaii rainbow license plates, and drove the three miles to the Honolulu airport. I hadn't seen my husband for six weeks and I smiled at the familiar sight of him, now walking through the double doors toward me and our new life in Hawaii.

"Aloha!" I yelled, much too loud for the taste of those standing near me, but I couldn't have cared less. The dimple on Brian's left cheek was apparent from across the airport lobby as he smiled and picked up his pace walking toward me. I greeted him to our new home with a deep purple lei and plenty of honi honi (kisses).

"We live here now! Can you believe it!?" I felt like a child on Christmas morning as we stepped out into the warm Hawaiian breeze, talking about how lucky we were that this was now our reality. We, Brian and Ashley, who had first dated fifteen years earlier, were together, now living our dream life, in a dream location, with our two children in tow. Our entire relationship, Brian had been gone more than he'd been home, deploying or traveling for work nearly two weeks of every month for years, so as a family, we were very much looking forward to our first shore duty assignment and having the time and opportunity to pursue our interests.

"Do we have plans this weekend? Can we get a babysitter and go diving?" Brian smiled; he was just as anxious as I was to get in the water. We had both fallen in love with scuba diving since our very first splash in those same Hawaiian waters and had goals of diving in locations throughout the world. Brian's personal goal list included diving each of the Hawaiian islands and to use a portion of his military GI bill to take advanced scuba diving lessons and pursue technical diving, specifically learning the closed circuit rebreather and how it worked. He did a lot of research about the different systems currently on the market, eventually finding a dive center, and an instructor, on the island that offered what he was looking for, and he was elated to meet with the dive school representative and realize this goal of his was about to become a reality.

One month after Brian met us in Hawaii, we found out we were pregnant with baby number three. We were excited, but cautiously optimistic. A few months prior, while still living in Gig Harbor, I became pregnant but suffered a miscarriage around the ten-week mark. That first miscarriage was devastating, to say the least. Brian and I had always talked about having three children, but when I began bleeding a week after seeing the baby's heartbeat for the first time, I knew deep down that something was wrong.

"It'll be OK, babe, let's call the advice nurse and see what she says before you worry, OK?" Brian tried to calm me down, but there was no use. I knew what we were about to find out.

Brian called the Navy after-hours nurse line while I lay in bed next to him weeping. I wasn't in physical pain, but I could feel our baby slipping away from us and I was heartbroken. We had already seen its heartbeat and we had started talking about potential names. *Atticus? Asher? Evelyn?* To us, this baby was already a part of our family and as the advice nurse told us to come in to get checked out, that vision was now fading away. Brian stayed home with Izzy and Hudson, who were both sound asleep, and I drove myself to the labor and delivery department of the same hospital I had previously delivered both of our kids. I watched in silence, tears streaming down my face, as the ultrasound tech scanned my abdomen. The heartbeat Brian and I had seen for the first time only days prior was now nowhere to be seen. I wanted that tiny heartbeat back, it had to be there. I wanted to beg the tech to keep looking for the heartbeat. I needed to see that bright little light pulsating on the black and white sonogram screen. It had to be there. I needed it to be there. The tears rolled down my face. My heart continued to break. Lying there by myself on the cold table, my abdomen still covered in gel, I began sobbing uncontrollably. The tech left the room and said the doctor would be in soon. I reached for my phone and called Brian.

"We lost the baby," I cried.

"Aw, sweetheart, I'm so sorry . . ." He didn't know what to say.

I wept.

"I'm so sad . . . I just . . . our baby . . ." I held the phone to my ear, tears streaming down my cheeks, before I couldn't speak anymore. Silence now from both Brian and me as we let the news sink in. I could feel his sadness on the other end of the phone line, for me, for us, for the baby we had already gotten excited about.

"I have to go, the doctor just came in. I'll let you know when I'm on my way home. I love you," I said as I hung up the phone.

The week after the miscarriage was brutal. For myself, for Brian, and for our marriage. I didn't want to talk about it, yet I did. I didn't want to cry, yet I did. I felt all over the place. I wanted to be alone in a dark room yet be anywhere but the house. Brian was just as lost, mainly because, for the very first time in our relationship, he didn't know how to help. This wasn't something he could fix and I didn't know how to be helped. There are no words to describe the pain and insecurity, inadequacies and loneliness I felt after going through this first miscarriage. Eventually, Brian found a way to connect with me and together we began moving forward and healing, together. So, when we found out we were pregnant again, six months after our first miscarriage, we were reasonably cautious. Unfortunately for us, this one, too, ended in a miscarriage. However, this experience was a bit less excruciating for me, for us, because we had been through it previously and just like every other obstacle in our lives, I knew we could, we would, get through this as a couple.

We got through this second miscarriage and enjoyed the next few months of island life, making our friends and family back home jealous with photos of our incredible adventures and sun-tanned bodies. Brian would ride his bike the three miles to work at Pearl Harbor and I'd take extended lunch hours from my own work and meet him for lunch or coffee dates. We spent our afternoons splashing in the low tides of Dog Beach or laughing at the kids from our front porch as they cooled off in their flimsy plastic kiddie pool, backs turning brown from the warm sun beating down on them. Brian and I relished this time together, our family, our ohana, soaking up every moment of Hawaiian life.

We watched on social media as the seasons changed across the country, summer turning to fall and leading to winter. Soon, we were looking at photos of our nieces and nephews playing in the snow. We'd be standing in line for Hawaiian shaved ice as cozy images of our friends wrapped in flannel scarves and puffy jackets appeared on our phones. Winter in Hawaii is not the same as winter everywhere else, and it's hard to get in the holiday spirit when you're spending your afternoons boogie boarding instead of building snowmen! But our winter was made even better when Linda, my former coworker at the bank in Washington, told me her husband, who is in the Air Force, received orders to the same base we were stationed at and they would be joining us soon. I couldn't have been happier. Linda has always been a dear friend of mine, one who has witnessed my relationship with Brian for years and was there for me through so many ups and downs of military life, especially as a brand-new military spouse. Having her come live in Hawaii felt as if a piece of home and comfort had just been added to our amazingly exotic and adventurous life. Our kids already knew her as Auntie Linda, so we knew they'd be excited to have her around.

We knew our first Christmas in Hawaii would be special no matter what, however, upon returning home from a family trip to the neighboring island of Kauai, I came down with the flu on Christmas Eve.

"Go upstairs and get some rest, sweetheart. I'll get the kids settled and bring up grilled cheese and Top Ramen for you in just a bit," Brian offered, knowing I wasn't feeling well. He'd made this meal for me dozens of times over the years when I was sick, always putting his personal spin on it, trying to make it fancy for me, and always making me wish he hadn't. He loved to cook, and my sweet husband was very good at a lot of things, however, this was not one of them. Grilled cheese with a spoonful of garlic inside, Top Ramen with a healthy dose of onion powder and paprika mixed into the broth. He tried hard to take things up a notch by complicating simple dishes that would have thrived in their most simple form. I wanted to tell him I just needed a simple sandwich with Top Ramen, but I didn't have the heart to, his eyes beaming with pride as he delivered this gesture of love to me, waiting intently for me to take my first bite, anxious to hear how much I enjoyed it. It turns out I wasn't that hungry anyways.

By the time evening rolled around, I was feeling a little better and I didn't want to miss our Christmas Eve tradition of driving around with the kids looking at Christmas lights. We got Izzy and Hudson dressed in their pajamas before piling into the Subaru, driving the brightly lit streets of Honolulu, admiring the red and green lights adorning houses and palm trees alike. We laughed at the cutouts of snowmen in people's yards, faded in color from the hot Hawaiian sun constantly beating down on them. Wishful thinking. Hawaii has one season: hot. We made it an hour into our Christmas Eve tradition before I was feeling ill again, so Brian turned the car around and we headed home. I was confident that all I needed was a good night's sleep and I'd be on the mend, able to enjoy Christmas morning with my family.

As he'd done every year on Christmas morning, or any holiday for that matter, Brian woke me up, a childlike expression and voice to match, already excited for the festivities ahead.

"Merry Christmas, sweetheart!" He leaned over and kissed my forehead, asking how I was feeling.

"Merry Christmas, babe." I opened my eyes slowly, the bright Hawaiian sun already peeking through our blinds for the day, as I smiled at the sight of my husband, already wide awake and with a childlike grin on his face. If there was one person more excited than Izzy and Hudson on Christmas morning, it was Brian.

"Do you think it's too early to wake the kids?" Brian asked as he jumped out of bed, searching through his pile of clothes on the floor. "I want Hudson to see his workbench and Izzy's going to freak out when she sees her bike!" He found the sweatshirt he was looking for, pulled it over his head, and stared at me with his bright blue eyes.

"You're ridiculous." I laughed as I got out of bed, heading for the door and down the hall as Brian walked toward the kids' rooms. I was downstairs filling our "His" and "Hers" mugs with fresh black coffee when the baby monitor next to me crackled to life, Brian's muffled voice saying, "Hudson, wake up, bud! Santa came last night!" Silence. "Hudson . . . Hudson. Hey bud!"

I could feel the excitement in Brian's voice and could picture him kneeling next to Hudson's white toddler bed, Thomas the Train blankets covering his head of curly blond hair. "Santa came, bud!" Brian tried again, this time getting met with a very sleepy "Mmmm." At which time from the assortment of sounds coming through the monitor, I could picture him lifting Hudson out of his bed and carrying him down the hallway toward me. I picked up my cell phone and walked to the base of the staircase just in time to see Izzy making her way down, her sun-bleached blonde hair and tan skin in stark contrast with her favorite blue My Little Pony pajamas. Brian, with Hudson still in his arms, was right behind her as I filmed the three of them walking toward me, a look of wonder and excitement overtaking Izzy's face as she saw the Christmas tree and surrounding presents for the first time.

"Oh my gosh, it's perfect!" Izzy exclaims into the camera, her three-year-old voice beyond excited about the display in front of her.

Brian looked at me, I looked at Brian, and we both grinned ear to ear.

Hudson, waking up now, wiggled free from Brian's arms and followed suit behind Izzy, running to the yellow plastic workbench Brian had stayed up late assembling for him the night before, inspecting every tool and gadget, seemingly taking inventory of his new toy.

"Cheers," I said, handing Brian his cup of coffee.

"Cheers, sweetheart. Merry Christmas," Brian responded as we clinked our mugs together and shared a quick Christmas-morning kiss before turning our attention back to the kids and the mess of wrapping paper and Amazon boxes that were now in front of us.

Forty-five minutes into our festivities, with Hudson's attention on a bright red fire truck and Izzy curled up in Brian's lap reading her new *Frozen* book set, I began to not feel well again. It was Christmas morning and I had wanted to enjoy this time with my family, but it was a losing battle and I needed to get back in bed.

"Go lay down, babe, I've got this and I'll bring you something up to eat in just a little bit," Brian offered, seeing that I wasn't feeling well.

"I don't think I can eat anything." I cringed at the thought of another of his specialty garlic grilled cheese sandwiches. "But I will take you up on the rest." I kissed his cheek and made my way back upstairs to bed. I could hear the three of them downstairs, the siren of Hudson's fire truck, the excited sound of Izzy's voice as she asked her dad to open the packaging of her new Elsa doll; these were the sounds of Christmas morning, of family. My family. I lay in bed, savoring these sounds and feeling thankful for my family, wishing I didn't feel so gross, when my mind began to wander. Where in the world did I catch the flu? We'd been traveling the week prior, maybe from someone on the plane? The kids aren't sick. Weird. I even had a flu shot this year. I never get sick, especially with the flu. The last time I had the flu I was pregnant with Hudson. Before that, I was pregnant with Izzy.

We had suffered two consecutive miscarriages earlier in the year, the second miscarriage happening in October, only two months prior. I hadn't had any flu symptoms with either of those pregnancies, but, my mind continued to wander. Could I be pregnant? Was it possible to be pregnant only two months after having the second miscarriage? No? Yes? We'd had sex, plenty of it in fact, so I guess it is technically a possibility, but do I want to get my hopes up? This is ridiculous. I have the flu, I'm not pregnant. But what if I am? With both Izzy and Hudson, the flu had coincided with the beginning stages of pregnancy; what if this was the same, and the flu was now a good omen for a successful pregnancy? I ran several scenarios in my head before making my way to the bathroom and rummaging through our medicine cabinet for a pregnancy test. I had done this four times in just as many years and knew the drill.

Pee.

Wash hands.

Wait three minutes.

Positive.

Wait, what?

No freaking way.

This was the only pregnancy test I had at home, left over from the ones I'd purchased in October, so I couldn't take a second to confirm the results. I didn't need to though, I knew. Deep down, I just knew. We were pregnant and we were going to have this baby. I got back in bed, a lump in my throat, a blue plastic bowl next to me in case I threw up, but a smile on my face. Eventually I heard the sound of Brian working his way up the stairs. I smiled as he appeared in the doorway and crawled in bed next to me, putting his arm around me as I rested my head on his chest. This was the good stuff. The moments we lived for together. A stolen moment, hidden away from the kids, to just enjoy one another's company, blue puke bucket nestled between us and all.

"I love you." I leaned into the little crook where his arm meets his chest.

"I love you, too, sweetheart. How are you feeling?" He tipped his head down toward me, kissing the top of my head as I savored the moment.

"Mmm, I don't feel great, but hey, I forgot, I have one more present for you." I did my best to hide the smile creeping across my face as I lifted my head from his chest to pull open the bedside table drawer next to me. "Merry Christmas," I said, reaching for the positive pregnancy test.

He looked from my hands to my smile and back to the test as he registered what this meant. "What! You're kidding me!" He erupted in laughter. "I swear, my penis only has to look at you and we get pregnant. We are the most fertile couple, I swear." I savored his reaction for just a moment before he asked, "Are you OK? How do you feel about this?" He was happy but wanted to gauge my reaction before getting too excited, knowing what we had been through together with our previous two positive pregnancy tests.

"I'm so happy. I don't know why, but I think this one is going to stick," I responded, confident enough for both of us.

Four weeks later, I had recovered from the flu and we made the twenty-five-minute drive through lush green trees and winding roads up the Pali Highway to our first doctor appointment. Brian and I rejoiced as she confirmed we were in fact pregnant, with a due date of September 2018, and we both cried tears of joy at the sight of the little bright light that kept blinking, indicating a healthy heartbeat.

Chapter Fifteen

We spent the next month enjoying time together as a family of four with another one on the way. Brian began his rebreather dive training while I planned a family trip to Japan. Brian had work to do on the Navy base there, but he was able to build in a few days of leave to the trip so we decided to invite his sister, Nikki, to join us and turn it into a family experience and enjoy a new part of the world together.

Nikki, the kids, and I explored the city of Yokosuka while Brian worked for a few days, practicing our Japanese, *Ohayo Gozaimasu*, and shopping at the 100-yen stores for cheap souvenirs and trinkets to keep Izzy and Hudson entertained. Three days later the five of us were on a northbound train for Tokyo, where we planned to spend our last few days on the island eating vegetarian ramen, marveling at the cat cafes, and making memories together at Tokyo

Disneyland. We'd been in Tokyo only two nights when Brian and Nikki received a crushing phone call. Their dad was calling from his home in Texas to say he'd been diagnosed with pancreatic cancer and doctors had given him six to eight weeks to live. Brian and Nikki didn't have the best relationship with their father, but this was devastating news and we were soon making plans to leave Japan in order to get them to Texas to say their goodbyes.

Three days later, Nikki, Brian, and Hudson were on their way to Texas to say goodbye. This was an important moment in Brian's life and he came home more committed than ever to be a great father to his own son. Eight weeks after leaving Tokyo, Brian lay in bed next to me as he wrote his father's obituary, tears streaming down his face, considering his own mortality and how important today, this moment, now truly is because tomorrow may never come.

My father passed away from Pancreatic Cancer on April 18th at 60 years old. We weren't very close, but nevertheless he taught me more about life than I realized in the short amount of time we did spend together.

Looking at my dad and I's relationship through the lens of being a father myself has made me understand just how precious each moment is; we truly do not know how much time we have left.

Not only did my dad pass away, but the possibility of repairing broken relationships, restoring lost opportunities for creating memories and the ability to get to know one another as adults all died as well.

Show affection and love to those whom you feel deeply today. There may not be a tomorrow.

The hardest thing I've ever had to write was my dad's obituary. I put it here for all to share but also so that it pops up in my Fb feed every year. Please feel free to tag and share anyone who knew and loved Brian.
I love you Dad. Rest easy.

Chapter Sixteen

Life has a way of moving forward even after tragic loss, and we were reminded of this as we found out baby Bugge number three was going to be a girl! Brian had always loved the names Charlotte and Claire but after much back and forth—and me heavily resisting those baby names— he came up with Adeline, and I fell in love with it. Izzy, Hudson, and Addy. *Cute.* To keep up with tradition regarding our children's middle names, we wanted to choose something that was meaningful to us and reminded us of a place we kept close to our hearts. Adeline was forever going to be our aloha rainbow baby, so we wanted something to remind us of our time as a family in Hawaii and soon decided on Makai, meaning *toward the sea* in Hawaiian. Adeline Makai Bugge. It was perfect.

When we weren't at doctor appointments or spending late afternoons as a family splashing in the warm Hawaiian waters near our house, Brian was diving. He'd been in rebreather training since January, but due to constant schedule changes at the dive school, his classes were continuously delayed or rescheduled and he was becoming increasingly discouraged. He was one class away from the certificate he was working toward and was frustrated when he received yet another text message from his dive instructor informing him that class on May 19 would be canceled.

He pulled the white aloha pillow over his lap as he sat next to me on our red couch. "I'm so frustrated. I know you are too. I'm sorry about all of this. I know this affects you guys too and I'm sorry. I'm thinking about dropping from this class. I want this to be my career after the Navy and nobody here gives a crap." Brian was clearly serious, considering his options for seeing it through versus dropping it now and coming back to it later.

I listened to what he had to say, looked at him, and then did what I knew he needed me to do, what he'd come to depend on from me; I encouraged him to move forward with this class. To push through, knowing the end reward would be worth the hard work and frustration now.

"I know you're frustrated. I won't lie and say I'm not frustrated, but I know you want this. You're so close, just finish it out and then you can take a break, regroup, and go from there." I did my best to make sure he felt encouraged, that he felt supported by me, by his family, to achieve his dreams, which in this moment included getting certified as a rebreather diving supervisor.

He listened to what I said, looking at me with his deep blue eyes before kissing me on the lips and whispering "Thank you. I don't know what I did to deserve you, but I'm so thankful to have you."

The silver lining to Brian's class getting canceled on Saturday was that he'd now get to spend the day with us! Izzy, Hudson, and

I had plans to celebrate Keiki Day, a children's festival held at Queen Emma Summer Palace on the windward side of Oahu. We hopped in the car as Brian drove us along the familiar sights of the Pali Highway, winding up two lane roads through the rain forest before arriving at the historic grounds. We spent the morning making paper leis, watching the children's hula school perform, and laughing as Hudson and Izzy took turns at the wheel of the fire truck they'd brought in for the event. Brian snapped a photo of Hudson sitting on the yellow fire engine bumper, hose in hand, red plastic hat on before posting it on his Facebook page with the caption *My Little Man*. Brian was proud. And happy. I smiled, thankful for this family we had created together and also thankful his class had been canceled so he could create these memories with us.

When we got home, Brian checked his phone to find class was back on. Sunday would be a dive in the ocean followed by an afternoon at the pool. He kissed me goodbye and left for the dive shop to have his air tanks filled while I took the kids out for frozen yogurt to celebrate the end of another beautiful day spent in Hawaii—and to cure my pregnancy craving.

"Mama, can we go to the pool when we get home?" Izzy asked me.

"Mmm." I checked the time on my phone. "Let me check with dadda to see when he'll be home and if he wants to go. OK, kiddo?"

Izzy nodded and smiled, frozen yogurt dripping down her chin, as I texted Brian.

"Oh, can I come too!?" Brian asked. "Please wait for me to come home and we can all go!"

I read Izzy the message from her dadda, knowing the smile it would bring to her face. She and Brian had a special bond and

I knew she'd be excited to hear he wanted to go swimming with us too.

"Tell Izzy that I'll take her to the biggest pool in the world if that's what she wants," Brian said, and I could just picture the smile on his face as he typed it, just as excited to spend time with his Izzy as she was with him. Our kids were blessed beyond belief to have Brian as their dad.

The kids and I pulled into the driveway just as Brian rounded the corner of Bridges Street and his white truck came into view. We ran inside to grab swimsuits and sunscreen before piling back into the truck and heading the half mile to our community pool. Five minutes later Brian was giving Izzy rides through the pool on her boogie board while Hudson happily splashed next to them, laughing as Brian captured water in his mouth to spit out at him. I settled into one of the lounge chairs scattered around the pool deck, enjoying the sight in front of me, admiring my amazing husband, the way he made our children laugh. I pulled my straw hat down low, shielding my eyes from the fading Hawaiian sun, and rubbed my pregnant belly, excited about the fact that soon Adeline Makai would be here, splashing with these crazies in the pool and equally enamored with her dad.

We got home late, well past the kids' regular 7 p.m. bedtime, but we'd made incredible memories as a family living our best life in Hawaii and it was well worth a little lost sleep. I made a quick dinner and the four of us sat together at the table, smelling of sunscreen and recounting stories of the day.

"Why don't you go upstairs and relax?" Brian volunteered. "I'll get the kids to bed and clean up down here." The dishes could wait until tomorrow and I wasn't about to fight him on it. *Deal.* I kissed the kids good night and my swollen belly protruded from my shirt as I waddled up the stairs. Minutes later, I was already cozy in bed as I heard Brian happily chatting with Izzy and Hudson as the three made their way upstairs.

"Can Hudson and I take a bath, dadda?" Izzy asked, a smile forming on my face as I heard her little voice, knowing Brian didn't stand a chance against it.

"Of course, sweetheart. Go pick out your pajamas and I'll get it started." Moments later the kids' bathtub was alive with splashing water, an assortment of plastic toys, and two very suntanned blond children.

I listened as Brian laughed with the kids, recounting stories of the fire truck they'd seen earlier, of how Izzy had been brave enough to hold her head under water at the pool, and finally what they wanted to do the next day when he was home from his dive. Once the last of the bathwater and bubbles had drained, Brian dressed Hudson in his red, blue, and white Paw Patrol pajamas and Izzy in her favorite pink Moana dress before tucking them in to their beds and kissing them goodnight. I was nearly asleep when he made his way down the hallway to our room and curled up next to me in bed. "I love you," he whispered before my eyes were closed and I was on my way to sleep—exhausted, slightly sunburned, and pregnant, but incredibly happy.

At some point, he left my side and went back downstairs to get his rebreather ready for the dive tomorrow. The last class he needed to obtain this certificate was finally scheduled and would take place tomorrow morning, Sunday, May 20, 2018.

***

"Hello?"

"Mrs. Bugge?"

"Yes, this is she."

"I'm calling from the dive shop, there's been an accident involving your husband Brian, where are you right now?"

Pause.

Accident.

Motionless.

"I . . . I am . . . I'm home, what's going on?"

"There's been an accident on the dive boat I need to know your address I'm coming to get you."

"NO! No, no, no!"

"Yes, Mrs. Bugge, we are coming to get you. Where are you? Are you at home? Do you have your kids with you? We need your address."

"STOP! No, please stop!"

Chapter Seventeen

Memories come and go in visual flashbacks that are hard to control. It took him twenty minutes to drive me to the hospital. It took me forty-five seconds to run across the ER parking lot, leaving my one- and three-year-old in the car with this stranger from the dive shop. It took me six seconds to find the reception desk and catch my breath long enough to blurt out my name. His name. *Brian. Brian Bugge. My husband. Diving Accident. Is he alive? Is he breathing? Please tell me. Somebody. Please.*

I stood trying to catch my breath, people in the lobby now taking notice of the panicked pregnant woman begging for information.

"Please take a seat and somebody will come out to get you," she said gently.

"Please just tell me . . . I just need to know if he's breathing . . . Please . . ." I begged, clutching my belly, feeling helpless, hopeless. *Where is he? Brian? My Brian. What's happening? This isn't real.*

I somehow forced my legs to work. One foot in front of the other as they brought me around the corner to the waiting room. I looked up to six sets of eyes on me. I recognized one set as a dive buddy of Brian's, but who were the others? Why were they looking at me like this? What do they know?

"Tim?" I collapsed in the chair next to the one familiar face. "What's happening? Is he breathing? Is he alive? What happened?" I began sobbing.

"We don't know. It all happened so fast, we were barely in the water when all of a sudden he was being pulled out of the water and the boat was rushing back to the dock," Tim began.

The others in the waiting room began circling around me, wrapping their arms around me, watching me cry as tears streaked their own cheeks. At some point it clicked—this was his dive team, his class. The men and women who had been on the boat and in the water with him less than an hour prior and who were now telling me they had pulled him from the water and done their best to attempt CPR on him.

"CPR?" I cried out. "CPR? Does this mean he wasn't breathing?" I started shaking. *This isn't real.* This was my first confirmation of the absolute worst-case scenario that had been coursing through my head for the thirty minutes prior—since receiving the phone call.

I couldn't take it a second longer. I forced my legs to work once again, jogging back to the reception desk and asking again for help. "Please. I just need to know if he's breathing. Please just tell me."

"Nobody has been out to see you yet?" the dark-haired girl asked from behind her desk.

"No, please, I just need to know if my husband is alive," I cried, clutching her desk to maintain my balance.

"Let me call again, OK? Can I get you some water? A chair?" she asked, obviously concerned for the sight unfolding before her eyes. *What did she know that I didn't?* I stood in front of her as she picked up the phone.

"The wife of patient Brian Bugge is here, can you please send out the doctor to talk to her?"

The doctor, that's a good sign, right?

"Bugge. The patient in room one. Oh, wait a second, the patient in the quiet room," she whispered into the phone. Not quietly enough. I'd heard it.

The quiet room? Is this quiet room because he had an accident and now needs rest and quiet? Or is this quiet room because he's not alive anymore? I couldn't stop the thoughts from flooding through my head. I was no longer breathing. At least not consciously. The double doors opened. The doctor. *Is that the doctor coming toward me? Is that a security guard with her? Why is there a security gua— Oh no. No. No. No. No.*

Didn't make it.

Quiet room.

So sorry.

Call someone.

Family.

Dead.

Tried.

Baby.

Calm down.

Dead.

The next two minutes of my life are excruciating flashes of images. Screaming. Bloodcurdling screaming. A pregnant woman collapsing in the hallway of the ER. A doctor with tears in her eyes saying "Sorry." A woman with blonde curly hair. *Does she know Brian?* Cold tile floor. Weightlessness. *Am I being carried?* "Your babies need you." *Who's talking? Who are these people? Wake up, Ashley.* Linda. *Is that Linda? What's she doing here?* I called her on the drive to the ER. *Am I in the ER? What's happening? I don't feel good, where's Brian? I need him right now.*

At some point, Brian's dive team picked me off the floor and my next flash of memory has me suddenly in the quiet room. To my left, a table with flowers, tea, and a card: "With deep sympathy." To my right, a nurse, holding my arms and trying to support the weight of myself and my unborn baby. In front of me, suddenly, Brian.

"BRIAN! Noooo . . ." I broke free of the nurse holding my arm and sprinted the few steps toward him, wrapping my arms around him and collapsing on his chest. I had laid my head on his chest a thousand times over our years together, always savoring the feeling of my head upon his warm skin as his chest rose and fell with each breath. I held my head here and waited. Nothing. I reached my hands to his face, the familiar stubble grazing my fingertips, but this time not met with his lips as he kissed my hands. *This isn't real.*

"Wake up. Babe. Wake up. I need you to wake up." I felt the breath leave my lips, I felt the hot tears streaming down my face, I felt people moving around me, but there's no way this is real.

This is my Brian. He's on the bed. It's him. Those are his tattoos on his legs and arms. Where is that dimple? There is no dimple.

There is no dimple.

I can't control my tears. I grab his hand and crawl onto the bed with him.

He is cold.

Why are you cold? I need you to warm up. This isn't real. Babe. Brian. I love you. You need to warm up. This isn't real. I love you. I need you. Izzy and Hudson need you. I'm pregnant! I can't do this without you. This isn't real. You're my Brian and I'm your Ashley. You need to wake up. I need you. You can't do this. This can't be our story. Wake up. Babe. I love you. This isn't real. You promised me you're always coming home to me.

I spent the next hour of my life pleading with him. For me. For us. For his kids. He was so cold. I kissed his hands. I kissed his lips. I begged him to please come back. I couldn't let go. This wasn't it for us, we had a life together, a future. We were always meant to be together. This couldn't be the end of our story. I held him, I whispered in his ear, I let my warm tears stream down his face. *Please just warm up*. He didn't. He couldn't. He was gone. My Brian was gone.

Linda appeared at my side at some point, gently pleading with me to come with her. "Sweetheart, Izzy and Hudson are in the car. They need you. Ashley, you need to be strong for them."

"I can't . . . Linda, I can't. This isn't real. This is Brian. My Brian. Linda . . ." I begged. I couldn't find a way to accept this as a reality. I'd had terrible pregnancy dreams throughout all of my pregnancies, a few times waking up in tears from how real they'd been. This was one of those. It had to be. There's no way this was real.

"Ashley, you need to be strong. You have to do this. Izzy and Hudson need you. Your baby needs you," Linda tried again.

I kissed Brian again. The love of my life. The man who had changed everything for me. The man I'd created a family with and loved more than life itself. I wept as I took in my last memories of him, the last sights and final moments with him as I kissed him goodbye and pulled my hand away from his. "I'll never stop loving you." I had to leave. I wanted to die alongside Brian on that bed, but I knew I had to leave. *Izzy and Hudson?* They were sitting in the car with a stranger while I was getting news their dad was dead. *This isn't real.* Linda held my hand, grabbed me by the arm, and together we walked out of the quiet room, down the hallway, through the sliding glass doors and out into the hot Hawaiian sun. She held my hand as we walked toward the black Subaru still parked on the street, the same car their dad had driven down to Portland five years earlier to take me on our first date after reuniting, only Brian wasn't here and now I had to explain to his children, our children, why this time he wasn't coming back home to me.

Chapter Eighteen

The following days were a blur to me, but I remember having to be the one who told our children their dadda was not coming back home to us this time. I remember having to be the one who had to give permission to a team of experts to remove organs and tissue from Brian's body so they could be donated—Brian was an organ donor. I remember having to be the one to make arrangements for his funeral. Yet, all these events come in foggy blurs and echo sounds. After all these must-do's had been dealt with, I had to announce to friends and people following our story on social media that the love of my life . . . the love of my life . . . what words should I use? Had succumbed? Died? Passed away? Fell victim to a terrible accident? It took me a very long time to come up with the right verb to use. My brain was having a hard time telling my fingers what to type. Part of me felt like the moment I wrote it and clicked "Post," this was all going to become even more real. I wasn't ready for it. But I had to do it.

I closed my eyes.

Took a deep breath.

Bit my lower lip so it would stop quivering.

Opened my eyes.

Looked down at the keyboard.

Began typing . . .

I have re-typed this at least 15 times and I still can't make it through without tears streaming down my face. I don't even know how to write this, but on Sunday morning Brian was involved in a tragic scuba diving accident. He passed away in the waters he loved doing something he was passionate about. I have some answers as to what happened but it will likely be months until I know more definitively the specifics. I do know valiant rescue efforts were made by some of his dear diving friends and I'm thankful to them for embracing Brian this past year and more recently myself as we all suffer through this piece of time together.

To say my heart is broken is an understatement. It is shattered. It is resting on the ocean floor with my husband and I don't think it will ever surface. He and I knew how lucky we were to have found each other and we talked often about how love like this only comes along once in a lifetime and certainly not for everyone. We shared an incredible life together and beyond any other emotion I'm feeling right now. I'm just thankful I had the time I did with him and was able to embrace the impact he has made on me and my life.

He was my partner in every sense of the word and while he gave me too much credit for everything, he was the one who made things happen. He sailed his 36' sailboat across the Pacific. He was an accomplished and published photographer. He was a Naval Officer. He was training to become a rebreather dive instructor. He was a husband and dang fine father. He looked at our babies the same way he looked at me; with complete love and adoration and it just never left you questioning his feelings for you. Isabel, Hudson, and our daughter due in September will grow up knowing the legacy of their father and the incredible man he was.

Conclusion

May 20, 2019
Oahu, Hawaii

The sun is caressing my face in a warm and reassuring touch. The salty air coming from the ocean is holding me in a comforting embrace, and the light breeze is whispering *E Komo Mai* in my ear. Today marks the one-year anniversary of Brian's passing. Our children, Isabel, Hudson, and Adeline are giggling and building sand candles.

Today is the day Brian is reunited with the waters he loved so much.

About the Author

Ashley Bugge is a military widow-turned-author whose writing has been featured in Military Spouse Magazine and whose story of turning tragedy into triumph will leave you feeling inspired to do the same. Ashley uses humor and personal tales of adventure, travel and chaos to tell her story of love and eventual loss as she becomes a pregnant widow at the age of thirty-four.

Ashley currently resides in Washington State with her beautiful three children and trusty rescue mutt, Chance. She spends her days hiking, writing, looking for budget-friendly travel destinations, listening to Rod Stewart songs on repeat, and shuttling kids back and forth to after-school activities.

You can read more about Ashley and what's next at: www.ashley-bugge.com

Appendix

Stay Gold

July 6th, 2017 – July 27th, 2017

Gig Harbor, WA to Honolulu, HI

www.svstaygold.com

Thoughts and musings written by Captain Brian J. Bugge while out to sea on his incredible sailing adventure across the Pacific Ocean. These were all written in real-time as trials, tribulations and triumphs were unfolding.

One Week Until We Sail Across the Pacific!

June 28, 2017

Preps are in full swing. Crew members arrive this week and next. Our departure is planned for July 6th at 10am – just a bit over one week. We are watching the weather closely and hoping the North Pacific High will cooperate. Right now, it's the blue circle in the image to the left. We want it to stay where it is, or a bit higher so we can sail nearly straight for Hawaii.

Stay tuned…more updates to follow!

Captain Brian and Stay Gold Crew.

First Day at Sea

July 7, 2017

First day at sea! We made almost 120 miles, leaving Gig Harbor at 10:06am on July 6th and arriving at Seiku WA at about 1:30pm. We haven't sailed at all yet; for a sailing expedition this has been a testament to how many times we can fill the Diesel engine fuel tank with 5 gallon jerry cans in a pitching sea without getting fuel all over (not many).

We have all been a little seasick, a little cold, and very much tired. There is something about being at sea that makes you only focus on the priorities at the time: keeping the boat moving and keeping yourself moving.

It's easy to forget to rest or drink or even eat, strange as it sounds. There are ALWAYS things that require attention on the boat so we are fixing small things here or there, or standing watch or resting. That's basically the routine.

Spirits are high and we had a great afternoon in the wonder berg of Seiku WA to fill up on fuel, food and brews. We are going to round Cape Flattery tonight and begin our long haul south along the coast. Make sure to follow us on the tracker!

Stay Gold,

Captain Brian and Crew

Grounded and Grinding it out

July 9, 2017

We are approximately 85 nautical miles off the coast of Oregon, heading southeast around a weak, unpredicted low pressure system. The past few days have been eventful. We are a bit tired and wet but spirits are high. It takes a lot to keep a sailboat running 24 hours a day, 7 days a week. We sail nonstop. To do that, we keep watch shifts. There are tons of ways to do this, we selected a rotating watch shift. We have to two teams, A and B. Each team has two members, Willy and I are in A and Beau and Chris are in B. Willy and I relieve each other and Beau and Chris relieve each other. We stagger the relief times so that there are always two on deck to sail and there are no gaps in turnover data. It's working well, but with this system and the number of crew members we only get four hours of time between shifts to sleep, hygiene, eat and write blog posts. It can get tiring.

I didn't mention this in my last blog post, but it's a good story to keep a guy humble and prove how it's important to work together as a team.

As we were coming into Seiku for fuel and brews we had to pass to the right of a breakwater. At the end of the breakwater was a couple of orange buoys (not official navigational aides) on the right and then on the left were docks with boats.

I cut the corner around the breakwater too tight and ended up soft grounding on a sand bar. As soon as I felt the boats motion change I knew we had grounded (done it a few times before!) and called out to the crew who was on deck that we grounded.

I immediately put on a hard rudder to turn the boat toward open water and the crew got on the rail to heel the boat. With the hard rudder and heeling we were able to get her off the sand bar and back out to the bay. I called the marina again and apparently they watched us ground and then get the boat off the sand bar. What's frustrating about this is that we had JUST called to confirm they had fuel – it would have been nice to get some local knowledge before we popped ourselves up on a sandbar. Also, I should have checked the charts better before heading in.

It was great to see the team hop to and get the boat back on her feet. Teamwork at its finest.

Time for a nap…until then, stay gold.

Captain Brian and Crew

An Albatross Kind of Day

July 9, 2017

The weather has filled in and we are making an average of 7-8 knots directly towards Hawaii. The latest weather GRIB shows the conditions should remain…we just need the boat and crew to keep up! We've made 160 nautical miles in the last 33 hours. Not too impressive as we had a night with very light wind.

I think the most stressful part of being at sea so far away from anyone else is the total trust you develop in your fellow crew and the boat. The noises that the boat makes are totally normal, but they make your mind wander. So far things are holding up. Stay Gold is a solid boat and she will take good care of us.

Earlier today we spotted a few albatross; a sign of good luck and favor to the sailor. It's believed that the albatross holds the heart of a sailor and they bring good omen. Let's hope so!

No luck fishing so far; we have a tuna handline ran off the stern and are trolling a huge lure looking for a tuna or anything else that will take it. We did see some tuna fishing boats out this far. We called one over the VHF to chat and he said they had only 15 fish for the day.

Our Raymarine autohelm is out for the count…it was working after factory repairs but after we got through the Straits it started to malfunction. I haven't been able to get it to work since. The selfsteering windvane is also a no-go; we can't get it to cope with the conditions nor set up correctly so we've resigned to steering by hand for the remaining 2100 nautical miles. Not much else will make you a great helmsperson than driving a boat for 12 hours a day with quartering seas.

If conditions hold and we can continue the momentum we've developed we should make landfall in about 15 days. That said…a lot can happen between now and then.

Final thought from a conversation in the cockpit earlier today; if you ever want to discover the true nature of your character, climb a mountain or go to sea.

Until then, Stay Gold.

Captain Brian and Crew

Adapt and Overcome

July 10, 2017

We almost lost the rig last night.

It seems like these things always happen in the middle of the night. I had just laid down for a nap after my watch. I'm about to put my headphones in and I hear Willy say "Brian, Brian! We lost the backstay adjuster".

I hopped out of the rack and ran up topside in my shirt and skivvies. Luckily, no rain. Just salt spray. The seal that holds hydraulic fluid into the cylinder – essential part of the equipment – had failed. Our backstay was flopping around like a wet noodle. This is the wire that connects the mast to the stern of the boat; critical for keeping the mast pointed up and not somewhere else.

Willy and I quickly devised a plan using some dyneema, a block and tackle and other assorted parts and pieces to keep the backstay where it should be. Later today, Chris used his climbing knowledge to form a more permanent solution.

I was really impressed with everyone's cool heads and ability to solve problems under pressure. I feel like sailing is just a series of problems that require solving, along with some wind and sails. Compound that issue with minimal sleep, dead batteries and the inability to run the engine to charge them (charging up now with solar!) and last night could be considered a kick in the balls.

Sun is out now and we are slowly making our way to the South-South West. The water is so blue out here, it beautiful. No whales or dolphins yet though.

Getting a few mins of sleep before my watch…Capt Brian

Netflix and Chill

July 10, 2017

This past day has been quite interesting. I asked Chris if he was having fun earlier and he looked at me with a funny look on his face and said "this isn't exactly watching Netflix and eating popcorn".

I rephrased the question "Is this worth it so far?".

He replied "Absolutely."

He's right though, this isn't the traditional definition of fun. Taking a boat 2500 miles across an ocean isn't Netflix and Chill. It's work. But, not to sound trite, nothing good comes easy. So, we grind it out. We solve problems as they come.

We started today down two on the scoreboard; malfunctioning backstay and dead batteries. We ended today with a jerry rig on the backstay that should get us all the way to Honolulu and the engine running, charging the batteries. Back to even. Thank some smart scientist for solar panels.

There were conversations early this morning about how we could make our way to the coast to pull the boat in to get it fixed. We decided to rely upon ourselves and fix the issue. This is why we are out here. Regular guys "facing up".

Speaking of regular guys. As I type this out on my iPhone I'm in the cockpit of Stay Gold with Beau, who has the helm. We are watching the sunset on a beautiful Pacific night and working our way to the Tropics (we have to steer by hand).

Beau is the definition of a regular guy. He's a 5th grade school teacher from San Diego who loves adventure and travel more than most. He once spent 6 months in New Zealand with 10 of his friends just for fun. When I called him a year and a half ago to see if he was interested in this voyage he said "ahh man I'm not sure, I don't really know how to sail or anything. Lemme think about and I'll call you back"

Not even five minutes later he called me back to say "Heck yes. I'm in." And he's been true to his word. He took an ASA 101 class that I taught the other day and then hopped on the boat for Hawaii. He's a natural at sailing and a great crew member.

I think what is most remarkable about Beau is how much of a team player he is. He started this adventure out of his element but wants to learn, doesn't complain about anything and is a joy to be around. We are lucky to have him.

It's about my time to take the helm. From the middle of the Pacific, with love...

Stay Gold and her crew.

11 July, 2017 16:47

July 11, 2017

[We are Loving the Support!!]

We are getting word from shoreside that there is interest in the updates from sea. We are honored and appreciate the support! We are just four regular dudes going for our dreams. It's amazing to watch people be supportive of that. If we can inspire just one person to take that step towards their dream then it's worth it.

Communication out here is limited, we don't have internet so we can't see comments on the updates but we can email. If you're interested in asking a question that we can address through the blog updates, feel free to email brian_staygold@myiridium.net and we will do our best to answer them.

Today has been a relatively chill day. We did some battery maintenance and cleaning during a calmer period of the morning. Always work and cleaning to be done. Between sail configuration changes, cooking, standing watch, maintenance, cleaning; the day goes by quickly.

We haven't seen another boat for three days. No whales or even birds out here. We are about 265 miles from land, just south of the Oregon/California border. In two days we should reach the same latitude as San Francisco and then head more west towards Honolulu.

The weather has been great, spirits are high, a toast was had crossing into California…we are on a roll.

Shoot us a question, like and share our posts! If you're feeling really froggy, we have Stay Gold gear for sale on the website… check it out!

With love,

Brian, Chris, Willy and Beau

12 July, 2017 11:40

July 12, 2017

[210! 210! Get the bow down!]

Friends! Wow…the responses to our blog and Facebook posts are amazing. We feel the love! Thank you for responding and for sharing/liking our posts! Keep 'em coming! I've received a few emails and Ashley has been forwarding us some as well so that we can get your feedback. Feel free to email your burning questions to brian_staygold@myiridium.net.

The past day has been much more relaxing than the first week. Part of it is that we are getting into a good groove. The weather has held and the winds are strong enough for us to make great time. We have become very fond of the course 210 – you tend to find lots of things to love about it after hours and hours of staring at compass in the dark of night. You make up songs, special names…there is even talk of some serious commitment to 210. Possibly in the form of a tattoo. Nevertheless…spirits are high, rum rations are not low and we march on.

Right now we are passing over the Mendocino Escarpment. I'm not an oceanographer and I don't have access to Google so that I can sound like one, but from what I understand it's incredibly deep here. On the order of 16,000 feet. That's deeper than Mount Rainier is high. If the vastness of the Pacific Ocean didn't make us feel small, that sure does.

This place is beautiful, yet desolate. No boats. No birds. No whales or fish jumping. All we see, day in and day out are waves. It's simple, yet can deal a lesson in humility quickly. Stop driving for 210 for a minute because you're wrapped up in a conversation about how Flare Training is a good idea and all the sudden you take a giant wave to the face. Regardless, we march on.

In response to your emails:
#1. For weather and communication we are using an IridiumGO and Predict Wind. Don't get a satellite phone and buy minutes. Total waste of time. It takes about 15 minutes to download a relatively useful GRIB file and that would cost $22.50, give or take, if we used Iridium minutes and a satellite phone. We have unlimited data with the IridiumGO plan and it works like a charm.
#2. There have been some questions on what each of us are reading. To be fair, we haven't had much time to read. But, when we do, this is the list: Brian: The Heart of the Buddha's Teaching
Willy: Blood Meridian by Cormac McCarthy
Beau: still trying to pick from his huge library he brought
#3. We do keep the sailboat running 24/7. To do that, we must keep watch at night to steer and also for a lookout. For the past week, we've been running a rotating 4 hour on/4 hour off watch section. Two of us on deck at a time. We have just amended that a bit so that we have a standby person who can read, sleep, eat etc during the last two hours of their watch. So, it goes like this…Willy comes on watch at 8am and stands watch until 12pm. Beau comes on watch at 10am and stands watch until 2pm. Brian comes on watch at 12pm and stands watch until 4pm. Ryder comes on watch at 2pm and stands watch until 6pm…and we just keep going. The downside of this rotation is that we only get to sleep in 2-3 hour increments. If you've done that rotation for any length of time, you know that no matter what you do exhaustion creeps in. Couple that with a boat this constantly in motion (it takes much more effort to cook or even move around the boat), constantly requires care and cleaning – doesn't leave much time to rest, let alone read or play cribbage.
#4. The weather has been decent. At night it gets down to about 55 or 60, bit warmer now that we are moving south. It also

depends on the weather system around us. We all wear proper foul weather gear, ie: offshore sailing jackets with big collars and nice hoods, overall pants, foul weather boots, etc. We also wear PFDs with harnesses and tethers so that we can clip into the boat anywhere. If there were to be a man overboard, we would be clipped into the boat and that would prevent us from being lost in the dark of night in big seas. Trying to keep ourselves, our gear and the boat dry is a constant battle. Every is damp. Humidity hovers around 80-90%. Temperature, right now, goes between 61 and 73 deg f.

#5. Steering by hand requires great concentration because of the seas we are in. We are on a broad reach (steering course 210!) with the seas on the starboard quarter and also some larger swells out of the west. This causes us to head up into the wind when these large swells come and push the stern to leeward. The person driving (the helmsman) must overcome that pressure on the rudder and bring the bow back down. It's a constant battle…it's quite a workout actually. The boat is charging along at anywhere between 5 to 8 knots, sometimes surfing at more than 9 knots. We do have an auto helm on board, and Raymarine assured me it was fixed before we left but alas it died again right before we exited the Straits of Juan de Fuca. The self steering wind vane we have works, but we are unable to tune it with the tiller in use. That would require us to pull in somewhere. So, we've resolved to steering ourselves to Honolulu and holding our heads up a bit higher than the other guys who relied on a machine to do the heavy lifting. If nothing else, we will be pros at steering a sailboat by the time we've clocked off 2500 nautical miles.

I've also been asked to give a bit more details on the remainder of the crew (Beau was in a previous post). So here goes…

Willy Kunkle, First Mate

A professional sailor, Captain and musician, he splits his time between touring with his band The Builders and the Butchers and sailing the world at the helm of mega yachts for the rich and famous. You'll know Willy by his mustache and his easy going, good nature that draws everyone in. He's a seasoned sailor with over 20,000 nautical miles to his name. Calm under pressure, resolved and always with a smile on face, Willy has traveled the world and has a thirst for adventure. He's an absolute joy to have on the team. His sailing knowledge is incredible and has been drawn upon…we've all learned a few knots we didn't know before.

Chris Ryder, Navigator

A crack navigator, Chris also has lived, literally, all over the world. He has also climbed most of the major peaks from Russia to Iceland during his time as a climbing expedition guide. He's turned his attention to sailing has his next challenge to conquer. When Chris tells a story about his life, it may seem like a tall tale at first, but he's got nothing to prove as he's done most of it. So, it's just best to let the story unfold and take it all in. Sometimes critical, always a realist and quick to question my dumb ideas; he's the keel on the team that keeps the mast and sails pointed toward the sky.

Brian Bugge, Skipper

Husband, father, currently a USN Chief, (soon to be) USN Naval Officer, photographer, scuba diver, USCG licensed captain and ASA sailing instructor. With a love of all things related to the ocean, sailing and a Transpacific ocean voyage feels like something I was destined to be a part of. When I'm not crossing oceans either on my own or for my career with the Navy, I'm exploring foreign countries with my wife and kids and doing my best to live life to the fullest (one life to live!). My goal in life is to never have a bucket list, instead completing adventures in life as opportunities arise.

Please continue to share our story as we believe that inside each of us exists an explorer, an adventurer, an expedition waiting to happen. What that looks like for you will be different than what it looks like for us. But, if we can do this, you can chase your dreams too. It just takes the first step…

Until then, steering 210.

<3

Stay Gold and her Crew

Pour One Out for an iPhone Lost at Sea

July 13, 2017

We are fighting for wind.

Who would have thought that 500 miles west of San Francisco, 800 miles south east of Cape Flattery and 1600 miles from Hawaii there would be no wind. The seas are flat, undulating, mesmerizing – but wind-less.

The decision was made late last night to turn the engine on and motor when the winds died off early this morning. We knew they were going to die off because we have been regularly pulling down GRIB** files from Predict Wind. It's a weather routing/forecast service that provides highly accurate weather charts and forecasts. I'm really happy with how it's performing, we've been able to use it with a large degree of accuracy.

We are moving south, under motor, at about 4-5 knots, in flat seas with a west swell. No wind. Just diesel exhaust and engine noise. Besides Willy kicking my butt in cribbage, todays big math exercise was calculating how far we could get with the amount of fuel on board and what time we would arrive there which would tell us if/when we will find wind. We have about enough fuel on board to make it 200 miles which puts us on the same latitude as Santa Barbara…the forecast predicts there will be wind. We shall see. If there is no wind between here and there, then we will have to wait until about Saturday for the wind to fill in. Once we hit the trade winds we should start crank out the miles again.

The quiet conditions gave us time to do some cleaning of the boat (one small head + four dudes = …well, you get it) and ourselves, sleep, read, play a few games of cribbage. We even flew the drone! Got some fun practice in launching and recovering, Willy nearly fell off the bow of the boat with the drone in his hands. Don't worry, we got the whole event on Ryder's phone. Willy scrapped his knee up, I tried to give him stitches but he insisted a bandaid would be fine. I was hoping to break out the suture kit.

The boat is holding up well. Having Willy onboard to help with maintenance and repair of small things has been awesome. We re-enforced the backstay today with some awesome teamwork across the board. Beau drove the boat like a seasoned pro and Willy and Ryder and I put our collective brains together to figure out how to get more tension into the backstay so the forestay wouldn't sag so much. It's easier to explain in person. In any case we used winches, pulleys, block and tackles and tons of webbing, shackles, lines and wire rope to shore up the backstay so the rig won't fall down when we hit the trades. Sounds much more dramatic than it really is. As Willy has said multiple times: "We won't lose the rig". I believe him.

I would like to take a moment of silence for Willy's iPhone. It's been committed to the deep, forever locked away with Davey Jones. Unceremoniously I might add…nevertheless, never to be seen again. Slipped out of his shirt pocket as he leaned over the rail to do something.

I have to give a shout out to Beau. I woke up early this morning, around 2am, to the sails swinging back and forth, no wind to fill them and figured Beau might need some help. He was up on deck, solo, at night, in the middle of the Pacific. You can hear the water, but you can't see it. There are no lights up on deck except the compass light which only serves to show you the course you're on. No lights anywhere else, pitch black. The water is hissing past the boat, you can't see the horizon, you have to trust your compass and the wind indicator at the top of the mast. This is about his 8th day sailing. Ever. That alone takes some courage. Beau has it spades. I make my way up on deck and find he's intently staring at the compass doing his best to stay on course. In this case, the wind had shifted and the current course wouldn't work for how our sails were trimmed.

I helped Beau trim the sails but could tell he was frustrated. I totally get it. Slatting sails in a swell take the power away from the "engine" and are super annoying to boot. You feel powerless. But, Beau, in his good nature was grinding it out. Not annoyed or frustrated, he was doing his best to support the team, complete the task assigned and with courage to take a solo night watch even.

Sailing, alone, at night in the middle of the Pacific can be overwhelming but Beau has taken everything this adventure has thrown him and turned into something positive. The first night we were slogging our way west through the Straits of Juan de Fuca; we had 20 knot winds on the nose, motoring against 4-6 foot wind waves that were 3-5 seconds apart (the boat was WET, cold and rocking like crazy). Beau took a night watch then and nailed it.

He has no shortage of courage and his good nature desire to learn is contagious. Beau Knows that he doesn't know but he wants to learn. I'm really happy how this crew has turned out. We are all working together, gelling and having a blast.

The past few days the weather has been overcast, even when we had wind. I was hoping to get a chance to see the stars with no light pollution, but it hasn't happened yet. Oh, from one Chief to another…a big shoutout to Phil Ryder for the heads up on Tropical Storm Eugene, we have been tracking it via our GRIB downloads and it seems to have died out. Tropical storms aren't such a huge concern right now, due to the time of year and how far north we will be but we are keeping an eye out. However, we really appreciate the heads up as I had no idea it had become a named storm.

If all goes well and we can crank out some miles in the trade winds, we should be arriving in Hawaii on July 25th, plus or minus a day. I want to make at least one 190 mile day…that's an average of 8 knots, sustained over the full 24 hours.

If you haven't followed us on Facebook yet, please do so! It's the best way to take part in this adventure with us. We are also on Instagram (@svstaygold) although I can't update that while I'm out here.

As always, we have crew gear for sale on the website – check it out!

Thank you all for sharing, commenting, liking and being a part of the great adventure! We are honored to share it with you!

Stay Gold and her Crew

**Gridded Binary Files are computer generated wind charts that we can use to forecast location, direction and strength of the wind. Crucial for success.

14 July, 2017 11:25

July 14, 2017

[Still motoring…]

We are still caught in this bit of a high pressure area. Pulled the latest GRIB and it shows we are close to making it into wind. We are able to motorsail right now which is helping with fuel efficiency. Gotta love those diesel engines. On 10 gals of fuel we can

run for 20 hours at 5 knots. Pretty good. We have a 4 cylinder 44 hp Westerbeke on board and she does a great job pushing us along. We have another 10 gallons of fuel on the rail for use, if needed. We shouldn't need it, by the time we get to the same a latitude as Santa Barbara we should be in the trades. I'll be happy not to listen to the engine run anymore. My head, when I lay down in my rack, is 3 feet away from the engine. Glad I didn't forget ear plugs.
Fifth day or so of clouds too. Nice cool balmy weather.
I think more cribbage is on the plan for tonight.

And we motor on…

July 14, 2017

Another day of motoring. It's getting old. We have to shout to talk to someone four feet away. I don't think I could realistically own a power boat. We all just want to turn the engine off and sail but the wind isn't there yet. This time under motor has given us the opportunity to relax a bit, charge our batteries and catch up on reading. Beau finally picked John Adams by David Mccollough. I'm working through True Spirit by Jessica Watson (thoughtfully gifted to the ship's library by Mark Watland during our send off – thank you!). Willy is reading Blood Meridian by Cormac Mccarthy and Chris is reading Adventures at Sea in the Great Age of Sail, edited by Captain Elliot Snow.
Rumor has it that tonight will be a crew dinner, tacos! We put all the fixings together, even have limes on board! Ashley made it work for us, she sneakily packed away some dehydrated taco filling… thanks babe!
Ashley is a big reason why we are here. She does so much to keep the family together, actually she does most of it. While I'm off playing boat, she's working a full time job, running a business

(www.mysouthsoundwedding.com), taking care of two small kids, getting a house ready to pack and move to Hawaii, being our unofficial PR Coordinator, getting cars ready to ship to Hawaii – she's insanely busy. And through it all, she keeps her head on her shoulders and takes it all in stride. I can't imagine how we would have gotten this expedition to where it is without her. There were multiple occasions where I was ready to quit, to sell the boat and give up. But, she pushed me on, gave me confidence, gave me the right thoughts to focus on and honestly, gave me the motivation I needed to push through the tough times. This project has encompassed our family for the past year and half. Not only were there countless hours working on the boat after work, but I picked up side hustles teaching sailing and shooting photography gigs to put extra income into the bank account to offset the costs of prepping the boat. The whole process is just too much to go into from a blog perspective, but rest assured, it has consumed our family in many ways. To see this dream realized is almost too good to believe. I've laid awake at night thinking what it will be like to sail in the middle of the ocean, with nothing around but the stars and the the sound of the waves to keep company – without Ashley and her tireless efforts, this endeavor would have never occurred. A debt I can never repay but I'll spend the rest of my life trying.

The big debate as of late is our heading. Maybe because it's the only thing that we can really fixate on, the thing that controls our destiny and short term future. We have some loose deadlines, for all of us, waiting on shore. We have business meetings and planes to catch…"real lives" to return to. Seems like it's so far off but the course we drive dictates whether we make those next events. Right now, we are heading south in search of breeze, but that's not making much way towards our final destination. Once this wind builds in, we can sail directly for Hawaii and start cranking off the miles.

We came across a pod of dolphins or whales earlier this afternoon, it was hard to tell. We thought they were Orcas at first but after they came closer they seemed like really big dolphins. Always a welcome sight to see a huge pod of whales in the same area as you. They didn't come really close, but we took that as a great time to hop in the water in hopes of seeing them…by the time we got it all sorted out it was too late to see them swimming. Regardless, Willy and I went skinny dipping in the middle of the Pacific and took a bit of a bath. The water was pretty darn cold, probably around 60 degrees but it was so refreshing. Eight days without washing besides wet wipes makes for dirty dudes. The water out here is so blue, it's such a perfect shade, it's the same color as the iMessenger icon on your phone. It's crystal clear and it feels like you can see all the way to the bottom of the ocean. I took a few minutes to scope out the bottom of Stay Gold, she's clean and in good shape.

After a few games of cribbage with Willy it's time for my watch. Spirits are high as we're about to hit the trades and start cranking out the miles (Havana Club helped too!).

Until then…Stay Gold.

One life…

July 15, 2017

At the helm of a sailboat, solo, at night, plying the waters of a vast ocean; you have some time to think about things.

Often, I wonder why we, as humans, do the things we do. We all chose different paths and put our energy into such different things. Some people find comfort in faith, others science, still others chose to just care about nothing. Some are extreme athletes and others won't take the elevator because it moves too fast.

Some people are fine sitting on the sidelines, at home, watching the tele all day. Others can't fathom spending more than a few minutes wasting time. When I talk about my families current adventures, I hear, all the time, oh wow! That's so exciting, that's on my bucket list! Or, what a trip of a lifetime!

I find those phrases, most likely offered with the purest of hearts, to just be things we say and mostly empty gestures. Like, "hey! How are you?" Let's be honest for a moment, when you ask someone how they are, nine times out of ten you've moved on to what you're going to say next before they've had a chance to tell you how they are. We don't live in the moment. We live so wrapped up inside our own heads that we don't always see what is happening around us. Most of the time, what is happening around is that we are letting life slip by. One life to live. That's it.

I don't have a bucket list. I don't have a trip of a lifetime.

Those are too temporal for me. Every trip is the trip of a lifetime because that could be the last trip I go on. We are halfway across the Pacific and I'm already thinking about what the next adventure will be…how to continue the Adventures of Stay Gold. A bucket list insinuates that we have time to do things before we die. We don't. We only have one life and it's fleeting. It's gone before we know we even have it. Today is your life. Tomorrow may never come.

Spend today watching the tele. Or spend today working towards your life's goal. The choice is yours and yours alone. You are the captain of your ship. Make it happen.

Hellen Keller said "security is mostly a superstition. It does not exist in nature, nor do the children of men as a whole experience it.

Avoiding danger is no safer in the long run than outright exposure. Life is either a daring adventure, or nothing."

Be afraid of stepping out and expect to never leave the spot you're standing on.

If you're one of those people who are comfortable sitting on the couch watching sitcoms and can be happy with that; more power to you.

But, if you, in your heart, know there is something you want to do with your life and are searching for the courage to step out on the road less traveled – here is your chance. If I can take a boat, over the course of a year and half and get it ready to sail across the Pacific, then actually execute that voyage – you can do whatever is in your heart. There is nothing in me that you don't have. You just have to make it happen.

What is in your heart, your expedition, your voyage, that you want to make happen? Leave a comment and let us know. We are here cheering you on!

Until then, Stay Gold.

Captain Brian

Freeloading Turtles…

July 16, 2017

What a day. We started out with little wind and a split faction of crew members vying for their vote on the course to sail. Some said south, some west. Southwest just wasn't an option with the wind direction coming from 065 True. That meant sailing 240 True was dead down wind.

We tried the spinnaker, we tried just one headsail. We tried gybing back and forth on different tacks but that required us to sail more distance overall, even though we were sailing faster. Each one of these configuration changes requires us to go up on the foredeck and hoist and douse sails and drag things here and there and winch on lines – it's pretty well straight up work. But…it's worth it.

We are almost in the Trades so we really want to take advantage of the wind and make VMG (velocity made good) towards Hawaii.

Willy saves the day. He comes up with this thing he did to sail across the Atlantic. The Twizzler Rig. No, the Tizzle Sticks. That's not right. Twiddle Sails. Whatever it's actually called, it's a twin headsail rig. No main, just two head sails, one poled out. I had heard of it before but never used it. Never heard of the name he called it but who cares. The crap works GREAT. We are cranking out the miles heading straight for a Diamond Head! Stay Gold, being and IOR boat can be a bit squirrelly dead downwind and can start this rolling effect so that keeps us on our toes.

We were stoked on Willy's awesome idea. But, to be fair, this was after Willy took a deuce in the turtle (we aren't 100% sure it was Willy, but who's counting). The "turtle" is a bag that holds the spinnaker. It's a big square bag, like a duffel bag. It gets strapped to the rail with the spinnaker in it and then hoisted from that so it's contained during the process. The bag fell overboard on the starboard side, but was clipped into the lifelines so it wasn't lost, per design. Normal for it to do.

We were sailing under the kite for a good while and Chris decided to get some footage of the the spinnaker flying. He went forward to film and looked over to see the Turtle swimming in the ocean with a few free loading passengers along for the ride. We surmise, the head is on the starboard side as well as the head overboard discharge…we were on a port tack which means the starboard side (head and Turtle) was lower in the water and made for an unavoidable circumstance. All is well after much cleansing of the Turtle.

There is one more crew member you haven't been introduced to yet. His name is Skip. I've been holding off because he's a bit of a freeloader and quite frankly none of the other crew are too happy with his performance. At this point, we just tolerate his ridiculous behavior. He's gotten a free tour of about 1,000 miles of the North Pacific and hasn't done much to earn the privilege. Despite his small stature and relatively bad looks, we have kept him around with the hopes he will do something worthwhile. To be fair, we drag him about 100 feet behind the boat 24 hours a day so probably feels a bit left out. If he starts talking trash after we get back, just take it with a grain of salt. After all, we haven't caught a single fish yet!

We are looking at about 8-9 more days…if the wind holds.

Until then, as always; Stay Gold

Breaking Necks and Cashing Checks!

July 16, 2017

We made it to the Trades!! Pineapple-tinis…here we come!

Flying Fish! That's Trade Wind Stuff!

July 16, 2017

Happy Birthday Beau Beau!!! It's a tradition, on ones birthday, at sea, to have to commit some heinous act of self disgrace to appease the gods of the deep. No need for them to feel as if we think of our "special day" more important than safe passage across these barren waters, their waters! It's typically up to the Skipper what the punishment will be…but it should be humbling. We do have that Turtle that could use a good scrubbing…

Nevertheless, all you land lubbers should feel free to wish Beau Happy 33rd Birthday! Not a finer way to pass a birthday than LITERALLY in the middle of the Pacific. We are 1000 miles from Cape

Flattery, 800 miles from LA, and 1300 miles from Hawaii. We are quite on our own out here. Well outside the USCG range to provide rescue, if we needed assistance it could possibly be airdropped but most likely it would come from a passing ship. Just a visual; we've seen three ships since July 7th. This voyage is just as much about preparation, seamanship and sailing as it is about self reliance.

The swells and winds are picking up to a spritely 20 with gusts to 25 knots. The weather was nice enough to stand my night watch barefoot with a light jacket on. We are solidly into the Trades.

We've made 70 miles in the last 9 hours. That's quick for a 36′ boat. We are able to keep a layline for Hawaii. Boat and crew are holding up well. We are in good spirits and enjoying the ride. Didn't get much sleep last night but Ryder will fill you guys in on why shortly. The bioluminescence in the water last night was nothing short of magical. As the hull cut through the waves it would leave a trail of brightly shimmering creatures on the waters surface. You could look out from the boat, in the pitch black, and see the crests of the waves as they disrupted the water surface what would normally be white water glowed in the dark. It looked like something out of a children's book; or another world even! So beautiful, it just reminds me how much there is to discover about the world we live in and how much of it is right in front of our eyes.

We've been visited by a few flying fish as well. We've passed orders to Skip to be on high alert. Time he did something useful.

Until then…Stay Gold

16 July, 2017 11:44

July 16, 2017

[Welcome to the Tradewinds!]

By Stay Gold crew member Chris Ryder

It's nights like last night that keep the expression "curse like a sailor" alive and afloat. Earlier, after much debate on whether to head south or west, Willy saved the day with his so-called "twizzle-rig" (2 headsails and no mainsail) which enabled us to run downwind on ideal SW course.

We were all enthralled with how well it worked...my only concern was what if the wind were to pick up? How could we de-power that much canvas quickly? Brian assured me that winds would remain stable through the night and thus I began my lonely 10 to midnight watch. With zero ambient light your only world is the dimly lit compass. That's the only data point you have to keep the boat running on smooth and on course; that and the jerky motions of the swells hitting you from every side. For one hour and 45 minutes of my 2 hour watch that's what I did, without any issue and making a good solid 6 knots. I was starting to look forward to some sleep when suddenly by beard filled with warm air...a lot of warm air...too much warm air for our little boat and that much canvas!

Within seconds I was reading 10 knots on the instrument and the boat was wobbling atop the crest of the swells, vibrating from the overpowering wind! It was all I could do to hold the boat from broaching (turning over sideways). I needed help from the rest of the crew fast as my biceps were giving out on the tiller. Since Willy had awoken to relieve my watch I saw him in the cabin and said, "Hey man, I think I might need some help up here"...a bit of an understatement, but we all feel bad for each other's lack of sleep these days.

We were speeding along dangerously (without seeing where to and whence forth) and we needed to get one sail down immediately. This is where the cursing takes hold...Chris, hold the $&@? boat up! Brian we $&:;?! need you on deck now! Turn on the @&£¥* deck lights! Everyone sprang into action (we let Beau sleep, because technically it was already his birthday).

I have to say, what followed was truly a sight…the deck lights over-illuminating Willy and Brian (in his skivvies) and myself pulling hard at the helm, the spray of the swells pouring over the deck. But we managed to get the sail down and de-power the boat, saving us from what was almost imminent at this point.

The aftermath was full of adrenaline-laden comments (££#*@&!) analysis of what had just happened. The warm winds on my beard? Yup, the trade winds…what a fine welcome.

Why Are We Doing This

July 16, 2017

I think it's a fair question to ask. Why, why spend all the time, money, sacrifice, burden the family, etc to make this voyage? Why sail 2300 miles across an ocean when we could have just shipped or even sold the boat. It's simple for me.

Because it's there. Because I have to.

If you listen quietly, intently, you'll hear a small voice inside telling you who you are. What you must do. The things that are most important. This is what I'm after.

I had to do this voyage, I've recently realized, because I needed to know who I am. This is a complex subject for anyone and not anything that can be surmised in a blog post. But, I think the why is important. What's the motivation.

The past 15 years of my life I've lived by other people's rules. Societal, relationship, jobs. They were very restrictive. I felt restrained. Confined. Never that it was possible to make such and epic journey such as this. That I was capable or worthy.

Ashley has encouraged me to live my life to the fullest. Not anyone else's. I didn't even know what that was until recently. We have kids now, bills, houses and cars. Mortgages. Surely it wouldn't be possible to undertake something as massive as crossing an ocean in a 36' sailboat. Her encouraging spirit has sparked my inner vision for who I am and what I want from life.

I can say with confidence; I am a sailor. Through and through. This is where I want to be. That's not the only thing that defines me as I am a proud dad and husband. Of course, I love my family, home, etc but – out here I feel alive in a completely different way. It's not better or worse than when I am with them, but it's where I feel alive in a different way. It's almost too much to put into words.

I had always thought I loved the sea, after so many deployments on submarines, summers spent at the coast, sailing around the Puget Sound. But I always wanted more. To test myself. To face up. Thoreau wrote "Men go back to the mountains and sailing ships at sea because on the mountains and the sea we must face up".

I felt unsatisfied; as if I knew I wanted to be a swimmer but was only able to put my feet into the pool and kick around a bit. How could I test myself, see if this really was who I am.

This past week and a half at sea have solidified who I am and what I want, personally. I want to sail. Be on the sea. It's so deep inside me it's undeniable. It's more than that though, seafaring will develop and uncover your deepest character strengths and flaws. That is where we find who we really are.

These revelations are the "why". That's what I'm after. I knew, instinctually, this voyage would define my sense of self and it had to happen for me to find satisfaction. Now, what's the next challenge?

Quick Update

July 17, 2017

We are running low on batteries and diesel fuel. It's a bit of a compounded problem. Sort of a chicken/egg thing. But, details are boring. So suffice it to say that if the sun isn't shining, our solar panel isn't putting out which means our Iridium Go might shut off. The Iridium Go is how we send our emails, SMS, blog posts and our updated positions.

In other words, if you see us go dark, don't fret. We are just waiting for the sun to shine.

In the meantime, we are safe, happy and making great time under spinnaker to the south.

<3,

Stay Gold and Her Always Posi Crew

Zen and the Art of the Spinnaker

July 17, 2017

The first week of the passage we stood rotating port and starboard 4 hour watches. The way it worked was Beau would come on watch at noon, I would come on at 2pm, Ryder would come on at 4pm and Willy would come on at 6pm. We would stand four hours of watch and then be off for four hours until your next watch.

This gave us two people on deck at a time, four hours of watch and four hours off. It was exhausting. You never get more than a couple of hours of sleep, maybe two. We switched to one person on deck and one on standby so the last half of your watch you can sleep but might be called on if needed. We try to respect others downtime as much as possible.

With this rotation we all stand solo night watches, under sail. It's magical. Seriously. There is something so perfect about sailing at night in the middle of the ocean, so far from anything and everything. I've never felt more connected to the sea.

These night watches give all the time to think. I brought an iPod so I'll listen to music which gives a bit of a "soundtrack to an epic movie" vibe for my watches. But, also lots of time to ponder.

The seas have been a bit confused lately and we will get bigger than the average ocean driven swells off the port or starboard quarter based on our tack. This tends to make the boat a bit squirrelly for a moment.

This was happening the other night and I kept thinking; "Man… these swells are terrible!". But the more I thought about it the more I came to the conclusion that there are no bad swells. The swells just…are. They exist. They are not bad or good. The wind moves along the water, far far away from where we are. The air particles create friction and drive the water particles. They energy builds up over time and soon you have a swell.

But the swell is neither good or bad. It doesn't care who or what you are. In reality, it's how we react to these swells that matter. How we trim the boat, configure the sail plan, react with the tiller. Those create a more peaceful, powerful boat or one that is unbalanced and noisy with a terrible motion.

The swells continue on. They don't change, for good or bad based on what we do. They just…are.

Things happen in life. Events occur. People say and do things to, for, against us. Those moments just…are. Swells come and go, but it's how we trim the sails and react that creates a balanced boat. I'm feeling very…zen…out here lately.

We've had the 1.5 ounce spinnaker up for most of the day, 10-15 knots of wind out of the NNE, small 4-6 foot swells out of the North. We are making about 6-7 knots, nearly due south. We are trying to get away from an area of high pressure coming in from the north. The weather is beautiful, morale is high, rum is running freely and we are on top of the world.

From the crew of Stay Gold, here's to your Monday being just as spectacular.

Going Dark…

July 17, 2017

We are low on batteries. Cloudy day today and not much power from the solar panel. Shutting down the Iridium to conserve power, so we won't be plotting positions on the tracker.

All is well. We witnessed a spectacular sunset tonight.

Will report back in tomorrow morning.

Until then…Stay Gold

Rough Days…

July 18, 2017

There is an aspect of spending time at sea that lends itself to an unusual sort of loneliness. It's strange, you're surrounded by people yet you feel this twinge of being alone.

Deployments on a submarine are where I've felt it the most. Surrounded by 130 souls and sometimes it feels like you might as well be out there by yourself. Here, it's a bit different. The four of us have grown closer and bonded over shared triumphs, toasts to victory and defeat. We tell life stories, we solve problems giving the celebratory high five after success. Living in close quarters, you grow close quickly. We are lucky to have such a great crew. One person who doesn't get along or has a negative attitude can throw off the entire vibe. Nevertheless you miss home, friends, family, etc. It seems to intensify about half way through the journey.

Today I was a bit out of sorts. Wasn't feeling myself. I've spent enough time at sea to know it was just a bit of a mental slump with some loneliness in there and didn't allow myself to get too wrapped up in it or make poor offhanded comments that could affect the rest of the crew. They noticed though, it's impossible not to. The best thing I've learned to do is accept it, try to work through it and understand it for what it is; just you mentally coping with a long term stressful situation.

This isn't fun like going to the amusement park. This isn't enjoyable like dinner at Applebee's (am I right Ryder?!). There are moments where those emotions emerge, but overall there is stress to cope with. There are problems to solve. There is a constant state of potential danger that exists. We aren't sitting on the sun deck getting served Pineapple Juice and Rum while getting our feet massaged.

We are changing sail configurations at 3am on a pitching foredeck. No one has showered in 12 days. We are eating dehydrated meals, nuts, bars and peanut butter and jelly. We are having hard conversations about pending weather patterns and the right course to steer to make landfall. We are managing interpersonal relationships in an environment filled with stress and the unknown; constantly changing variables. We are living, cooking, cleaning, sleeping and generally existing within a 10 x 15 foot space.

Today we passed south of 30 degrees North. We are, quite literally, 1000 nautical miles from civilization. That's about the same as standing in Seattle and having EMTs, the Fire Department, tow truck, etc somewhere around Minneapolis. We are on our own. The danger is real. There is no help around the corner. The USCG range is about 500 nautical miles from land.

This is a challenge. And it helps to recognize that. To embrace it for what it is. To mentally acknowledge that what we are doing isn't easy, but in the end will be an achievement and totally worth it. In the end, nothing worthwhile comes easy.

Even though it sounds like we are gluttons for punishment and I might be coming across a bit dramatic; we knew this what we were getting into. We wanted to test ourselves, the ship – against the Pacific. We set out to do exactly what we are accomplishing. THAT is why we are doing this, not because it's "fun".

We appreciate all the comments, shares, likes etc on our stories. It makes us feel supported! Keep it up! We will keep them coming! Also, just to let you know – we can't see the comments left here – no regular internet out here. Just email. Please don't feel like we are ignoring you because we haven't commented back.

Don't forget to check us out on Instagram: @svstaygold and check out our Crew Gear on the website!

Until then…Stay Gold

14 days and Counting

July 20, 2017

We are all exhausted. The past 24 hours has been busy. It started out last night with spaghetti night and then for dessert, a series of squalls running through which left us on our toes. After an evening sail configuration change in the rain and a squall, we went back to running straight 4 hours on 4 hours off with two on deck to make sure we could handle whatever came our way. This left everyone with a severe lack of sleep.

It seems like at night the weather picks up and that's when things get a bit hairy. In the morning, it calms down and then picks up again in the afternoon.

The noise and motion of the boat is such that when we are making good progress the boat is rocking and loud – when we are not making good progress it's easy and quiet – perfect time to nap. Oh the irony.

We woke up to a wet, humid boat. Always lots of fun. The rest of the day was filled with work. Willy and I got the engine started and charging the batteries but it only lasted for a few minutes then died on us. After troubleshooting we found it was a few dirty filters. I had two of the three spares on board but the most important one was taken off at some point and never put back on. Shame on me. The plan is to try to clean it out tomorrow and see if we can get it back to working.

Willy also re-enforced our backstay rig with a broken hydraulic cylinder I found in the recesses of the boat while searching for a fuel filter. He refurbished this old broken backstay adjuster and we put it on to attempt to tighten the temporary rig we have now. It totally worked! Willy for the win! He's a never ending array of knowledge and surprises. Super happy to have him on board.

Beau is learning how to be a killer helmsman. He calculated that we have all spent about 84 straight hours at the helm. Won't get that experience in a classroom. He does great though, locks in and gets it done!

By the time the evening comes we are all wiped out and napping or reading or standing watch. Not having an autopilot is a burden. As much as we will like to say we did it without one; I would NOT recommend doing this voyage without one unless you're racing. I will be ripping ours out and sending it back to Raymarine for a replacement. We purchased it specifically for this passage.

Today marks 14 days on board. We are all ready to have more personal space, take a shower, eat a good meal. The mental aspect compounded by the lack of solid sleep is starting to wear on the team. But, the experience is still absolutely worth it.

Time for a nap…until then, Stay Gold and Crew

Stay Gold Pony Boy

July 21, 2017

Today marks the 16th day of this voyage. Mentally, I'm having a hard time wrapping my head around that. Seems like we were just leaving Gig Harbor yesterday.

It might have something to do with the fact that each day is relatively the same. We stand the same watches. Have the same routine. The view consists of clouds, sun, sky, waves, the occasional flying fish and more occasional bit of random plastic.

Speaking of that. Fun fact; we have had our fishing line out for the past 16 days. We have caught one small Dorado. The guys fried it up for fish tacos, I abstained as I don't eat meat. Now for the sad fact: we have caught more pieces of plastic on our lure than fish. We have seen 10 times the plastic floating by us. We are killing our oceans. It's not an "alternative fact"; it's simply the truth. If you don't believe me, get in your boat and come out here to check it out. In the meantime, feel free to reduce the use of plastic and recycle. The flying fish out here will appreciate it.

Anyway, I digress. Stand by for a bunch of sailing jargon…The sailing today has been epic. Sunny skies, 15-20 knots out of the NNE. Swells out of the east at 8-10 seconds, Stay Gold is charging along on a broad reach, port tack, under a full mainsail and a 110% genoa, she's taking the swells in stride – this is her time to shine. She loves this weather, it's what she was made for. At the helm, she feels alive and full of energy, perfectly balanced. So much fun to sail. All those super light air buoy races aren't so much fun with a boat made to take on the ocean. Conditions like today make me proud of her and are just too much fun to sail in.

To wax philosophical…I've been working hard to learn the lessons that this voyage is trying to teach me. As I type this, I'm not sure which one I want to talk about as the past few days have been a quite the learning curve.

A big part of the reason for undertaking this endeavor is not only fulfillment of a dream, but to discover more about who my true character is. Without some level of adversity I won't be challenged to move out of my comfort zone and see who I really am.

I've learned, that sometimes what I find, after coming through a challenge is that I am not who I thought was, or at least my "self view" is a bit skewed. And I might not like the result. But that's a good place to be, I think. To some degree, that's where I'm at now and it gives the opportunity for growth and improvement, if that's what I decide to do with it.

I had set some expectations for what this experience would give me. Reality hasn't matched what I thought those expectations should be and part of my "suffering" is coming to terms with that. The interesting thing is, even though my unrealistic expectations aren't being matched, this is still been a life changing experience. Acceptance of what is, not expecting what I think should be.

We are getting close to finishing this adventure. I'll have to start planning the next one, earmuffs Ashley! Closing in on 600 miles left…we expect to make landfall on the 26th or 27th. In the meantime, thank you all for reading, sharing, liking, commenting, etc. We love it! Keep it up! By the way, we can't read the comments, no internet – just email. We will respond when we can.

Until then…Stay Gold

Can't Beat a Seawater Bath

July 22, 2017

Friends and family. As I type this we are nearing the 600 mile mark to Diamond Head. We are making a bit slower speed today to favor a more preferred westerly course. With the wind directly out of the north east, it makes it hard to sail with efficiency to the south west. We tried the Twizzle Rig (twin headsails – no main) but that puts a lot of pressure on the forestay which stresses the backstay which is being held up with web strapping and other assorted bits and pieces of gear. There is certainly a concern that the backstay or forestay could fail so we are avoiding the Twizzle Rig for now. Unfortunately that means a bit slower speed to our destination.

Ashley sent me a digest of some of the recent comments on the Fb page. WOW. I am so honored that you are all following along on our adventure. Thank you for taking the time to write to us, it means the world. I had no idea, when I set out on this adventure over a year and half ago that so many people would want to follow along and be inspired by it. I'm beyond pleased that is the case and sincerely appreciate all of your support.

Overall, we are doing well out here. The wind and weather is fair and we are making good progress to Honolulu. During the day, the inside of the boat gets around 81 with 80% humidity, so the ocean breeze feels nice. We are all getting a bit antsy to get off the boat, get some downtime, a good shower, clean bed and a few brews (it's the simple things in life, I tell ya!). The highlight of today, for me, was taking a bath with saltwater! Feels amazing not to have greasy hair. We can tell we are getting closer to civilization. Early this morning we had a huge container ship overtake us on the starboard side at about 2 miles out. I hailed them on the VHF, mostly cause it's fun to chat it up a bit and see what the deal is. Also to make sure they saw us and we weren't in danger of a collision. After chatting a bit they altered course. They were headed to Hawaii as well and confirmed our weather sources were correct with regard to Fernanda. It's nice to make a connection with other souls out here that aren't on the same boat as us. Makes us feel like the vast ocean is just a bit smaller. We've also seen a few aircraft flying overhead. Hard to tell what type, but they're not commercial jets. First signs of civilization after venturing through 1500 miles of uninhabited badlands. This ocean is so huge, it really makes one feel insignificant.

Quick update…

July 23, 2017

We are about 450 nautical miles out from Honolulu. Making an average of 6.2 knots, we have been putting down 150 mile days. Quite a bit has happened in the past 24-36 hours, but I'm not in a good head space to write it up for the internet. I'll fill you in later. In the meantime, its sunny, the winds are sassy (leftovers from Fernanda) and we are making good time under just a 110% headsail. Everyone is safe and the boat is doing well. Preparations are in progress for making landfall.

Recommend a Good Tattoo Shop in Honolulu!

July 23, 2017

Wow…what a few days! We are closing in on the 300 mile mark quick! The remnants of Tropical Storm Fernanda are giving us a bit of an extra push. We are making an average of 6.2 knots with just the headsail! Big swells out of the east today…some 15+ footers. Hard for me to gauge, I'm not the best at it. But they were big.

I spent today crafting a tow bridle and working with BoatUS to get a strategy down for getting into Pearl Harbor. We are having fuel filter issues and can't run the engine. Luckily, we have the solar panels which are providing a bit of power for our electronics.

We will need to be towed into Pearl Harbor which, to be honest, is a bit humbling after sailing 2500 miles. The engine is clogged with dirty fuel. It's probably a simple fix, just need the right fuel filter. But, I forgot to make sure it was on board before we left. It is always the simple things. In any case, we can't run the engine which is a pretty big deal.

Other small things have been breaking on the boat so we are coming up with ways to fix them. The compass light is going out intermittently, so we are using a clip on book light Lisa, my mother in law, gave to me for Christmas. Works pretty well. Willy has been the man with coming up with ingenious ways to fix stuff. He's always willing to hop into the bilge or engine to figure it out. Absolutely stellar. Quite a lifesaver to have on board.

Last night we had to reef* the mainsail in the middle of the night. It was a lesson in how quickly things can go wrong when we do them too fast in a highly dynamic environment. Simple process, but in the dark, with wet decks, and in a pitching sea things get complicated. The winds had picked up enough that we just wanted to run with a headsail alone as we could get a better course. Rather than talking through the process, we knew what we are doing after all, we just went to it.

During the middle of the procedure, I was at the helm, and Willy asked me to "head up" (point the bow towards the wind) as this would alleviate tension on the mainsail and allow us to reef it. Rather than head up, I accidentally beared away (put the stern through the wind) and we did an uncontrolled gybe. The boom swung from one side of the boat to the other and almost knocked Ryder into the water and almost nailed Willy in the head.

A very serious situation. Two things on a boat that can kill you; the boom and going overboard. Luckily Ryder was safe and no one was hurt. I felt terrible. We were close to a very bad night and really, it was my fault.

We got the main reefed and all calmed down. Needless to say, I didn't sleep well after that.

There have been so many lessons learned during this trip. Not just about sailing and the sea, but about life, about myself, about others. I'm still trying to digest all of them. But, one that has hit home since last night is that we all make mistakes and the key is to learn from them and become better for next time. I feel like this is a lesson I've learned often but life keeps teaching me. More to come on this…

In the meantime, we are making plans for our port call and which tattoos we are going to get to commemorate the occasion.

We are all safe and in good spirits; but certainly in need of a shower and a good nights rest.

Much thanks to everyone following along, this has been one wild ride (still some to go!).

Until then…Stay Gold

*Reefing a sail is a process where we make the sail area smaller thereby reducing pressure on it from the wind and lowering the center of effort on the sails. It's something we do in high winds to make the boat more controllable.

Friendships Are The Best Ships

July 24, 2017

I woke up this morning, after taking a short nap after my 0400-0600 watch and went topside to check things out. It smelled like Hawaii…we are still 250 miles away, but the ocean looks and smells like the ocean near Hawaii.

And yes, the Pacific looks different depending on what latitude you're on. Lots of different personalities.

It's been hot the past few days. Today was gnarly. 88 degrees Fahrenheit with 85% humidity. Fortunately, no major sunburns or anything of that nature. Beau got a bit toasty on his back.

Our navigation calculations show us arriving around 8pm on July 26th. Trying to make it a bit faster, so we can come in during the day. This is the last 48 hours of our epic journey. As much as we are all looking forward to getting a shower, good nights sleep, a couple brews and some time with family, it'll be bittersweet to have it be over.

The days leading up to pulling into port are always filled with anticipation and longing for the simple pleasures we don't get out here, but there is an adjustment to life on land just like an adjustment to life at sea. This has become our reality out here. We stand watch. We sleep. Eat. Fix the boat. Plan the passage then stand more watch. It's simple. Now we are already in the process of mentally preparing for adjusting to life on land. Talks turn not to sea stories or other general BS'ing, but to what we are looking forward to doing, eating, drinking etc.

We are all subconsciously preparing to become temporary landlubbers again. Until the next adventure.

The current plan is to sail to the north shore of Molokai, transit west until we hit the Molokai Channel then head south west to Oahu and our rendezvous point with the tow vessel.

If you're on the island of Oahu, you can see us transiting Molokai Channel on July 26th – probably around 4pm HST.

Thank you all for being a part of this awesome adventure with us!

Until then…Stay Gold

Big Island to the South!

July 25, 2017

We are just about at the same longitude as the eastern edge of the Big Island! That's pretty much Hawaiian waters, right?!

The wind is a bit lighter today so we are not making such great progress. We will most likely arrive tomorrow very late, maybe around midnight.
Everyone is having fun, enjoying the last bit of this experience. No sight of land just yet. It will most likely be Molokai first thing tomorrow morning.
See you soon Hawaii!

Land Ho!

July 26, 2017

At 10:06am, Hawaii Standard Time, Team Stay Gold spotted Maui forward of her port beam! We are getting close!
New plan is to take the Pailolo Channel to the south side of Molokai, then continue our transit west, keeping north of Lanai.
The weather forecast for today showed a small high pressure system just north of Molokai and we didn't want to get stuck in that.
We should be in the marina around 3 or 4am!

First Days Back in Port

July 31, 2017

After 21 days at sea, almost to the minute, the crew of Stay Gold has made landfall. Now, a few days later we have dispersed from the island to all parts of the world. Less than 100 hours ago we were prepping to make our arrival, still with salt in our eyes, wind in our hair and the sea in our hearts.
Coming home from sea is a strange transition. You'd think it's the opposite of leaving life on land to a life beating to the rhythm of the ocean but it's different – at least for me. After a decent period at sea, you become accustomed to your new reality. You learn to lean into it. To trust it. To enjoy it. It becomes warm and inviting, safe.

The boat is not only your home but your best friend. It's easy to see why sailors of the ancient times referred to ships in the feminine form – something we still do. It's because you grow fond of them. To love them. Look at them with affection. It might sound strange at first, but when you're 1000 miles from land in any direction it becomes clear.

Knowing landfall is approaching causes the ship to take on a different vibe. Talk shifts to what we will do when we hit port, what we will eat, drink. Concerns become land based, a mental aspect of shifting from sea-going to land-bound. Part of the transition. At first, I resist it. Then it takes hold and I long to see my family and eat a decent meal. It's not instantaneous though. For a week or so after getting back from sea I still feel like I'm in transition, but soon it passes. Very strange.

We hit port after a rough day and half passing through some restricted channels between Molokai, Lanai and Maui. The winds were compressed and contemptuous. The swells were frustrating and the wind waves pushed us around. Beau had to fight 30 foot breaking swells off Molokai and I had 35 knot gusts of wind pushing to boat to over 10 knots of sustained boat speed – but we made it. We hand steered 2500 nautical miles all the way across the Pacific.

We were towed into Pearl Harbor by Michael of Vessel Assist who did a bang up job of getting us into port. We had to be towed because I made some very simple, easy to fix mistakes (always do your maintenance on your batteries and ALWAYS have the proper fuel filters on board!). I've learned so many lessons, but feel free to learn these from me – maintenance is CRUCIAL. Even for your car. I'll write more about those later.

After hitting the dock we were welcomed be an awesome welcome home party, put together by my wife Ashley. Family flew in from all over to welcome us – very heart warming. It's bittersweet when an adventure comes to a close, but Willy, Chris, Beau and I have taken and given so much of this experience that even a book wouldn't cover it all. And that's quite ok. Some of what happened out there will always remain between the four of us. Maybe a book will arise…we will see.

For the foreseeable future, the crew of Team Stay Gold is going to tend to family and career obligations but will be back soon with a new adventure. I'll be writing more, as I can, to fill in some details of this story, so stay tuned.

We do want to thank Chief Phil Ryder, USCG ret, for his wonderfully colorful updates on Tropical Storms Fernanda and Greg along with his musings on life at sea from the East Coast. Also, thank you to Erica and Rich at Rainbow Bay Marina for helping us get sorted out upon arrival and during the trip. A hearty thank you to Eric for helping Ashley work out logistical details for the Homecoming Party and making her feel like part of the Navy Ohana. And, as always, thank you to our families for always supporting our dreams.

A VERY special thank you to Ashley for organizing a Bon Voyage and Homecoming Party, in two separate states. Ashley was also our outstanding Public Relations coordinator who worked with the Navy, multiple news outlets and other entities in Washington and Hawaii. She ran the Facebook page and talked on our behalf to families and others while we couldn't. This expedition wouldn't have happened without her tremendous support and self-sacrifice of time and energy. She's the heartbeat of the team and we love her endlessly for it.

Finally, a special thank you, to you, dear reader. As much a part of the team as we are, you gave this voyage an extra depth that wouldn't exist if we kept our adventures to ourselves. Thank you for following along, liking, commenting, sharing and providing encouragement. We hope you have been changed a bit, like we have, from the experience.

Again, please stay tuned as we have just begun.

Until then, Stay Gold

<3,

Brian, Willy, Chris and Beau

Printed in the USA
CPSIA information can be obtained
at www.ICGtesting.com
JSHW022216140824
68134JS00018B/1091

9 781642 799088